It's All About You

Ronald Terrell
and
Michael Terrell

PRESS

It's All About You
by Ronald Terrell and Michael Terrell

Printed in the United States of America

ISBN 978-1-60477-345-3

www.xulonpress.com

Table of Contents

Introduction

This book has been waiting for years to be birthed. The seeds for it were sown when our parents introduced us to regular church attendance and worship when we could barely walk. Coming from modest backgrounds, they realized some things transcend time, and a foundation in the Bible was one of them. Thankfully, our parents and grandparents sought that narrow path Jesus talked about and they set the example for us. For their early diligence, we are forever grateful.

We knew we wanted to build a book from those childhood seeds. The genesis of sharing our hope and vision was there; however, the nuts and bolts of writing were absent. Then, like a gentle rain sent to get the spring crops started, God sent us a lighted candle to help us see our way and make this book possible. Our intrepid editor, Phyllis M. Rees, recognized the potential of our initial efforts. With unbridled encouragement and the patience of Job, she helped us organize our notions and ideas, then married them to paper. Taking our scraps and remnants as we produced them, she guided us in piecing together a tapestry that shows God both in simple humility and grand majesty.

Whether you are seeking guidance or have a growing curiosity about the Bible, this book will meet your needs and engage your intellect, prodding you to seek your creator on your own. From finding unlikely heroes to faith's hall of fame, *It's All About You* will gently guide you into an appreciation of what God has done for you. This book belongs in the hands of every parent, teacher, minister, and leader. Included are lessons that are timeless and applicable to our daily lives. We want you to be impressed by the Bible all over again. Be prepared to read, study, and reawaken the gifts sleeping within you.

The authors have backgrounds in education and construction, and since Jesus was both a teacher and a carpenter, this coincidence did not escape the authors' notice. They feel privileged to walk in those special sandals.

Everyone should attend a church that challenges him to study and apply the Bible's truths to daily living. Southeast Christian Church in Louisville, Ky. is such a church. We are grateful for the impact it has made in our lives, our community, and the community of missionaries the church supports. The authors felt a need to give back something after receiving so much over the years. While writing this book, we had our family and friends in mind, but it is mainly about those who are seeking and finding Christ and those who are about to enter the Kingdom of God.

Acknowledgments

We would like to gratefully acknowledge the help and inspiration of the following, without whom this book would not have been possible.

Elah-*The Adorable One*; (Ezra 4:21;Daniel 6:23). El-Elyon-*God Most High*; (Genesis 14:18-22;Numbers 24:16;Deuteronomy 32:8).El-Roi-*The Lord That Seeth*; (Genesis 16:13,14). El-Elohe-Israel-*God of Israel*; (Genesis 14:18-23; 33:20). El-Olam-*God of Eternity*; (Isaiah 26:4; 63:16; Jeremiah 10:10;Psalm 90:2;Isaiah 40:28). El-Shaddai-*The Almighty, All-Sufficient God*; (Genesis 17:1;II Corinthians 6:18;Revelation 1:8; 4:8; 16:14; 19:6). Adon-Adonai-*Jehovah Our Ruler*; (Ezekiel 16:8,30). Jah-*The Independent One*; (Exodus 15:2;Isaiah 26:4). Jehovah-*The Eternal, Ever-Loving One*; (Revelation 1:8;James 1:17). Jehovah-Elohim-*The Majestic Omnipotent God*; (Zechariah 13:9;Psalm 118:27. Jehovah-Hoseenu-*The Lord Our Maker*; (Psalm 95:6;Exodus 12:47;Deuteronomy 28:1;Exodus 36:10-38). Jehovah-Jireh-*The Lord Will Provide*; (Genesis 22:8; 22:14;Hebrews 11:19;Romans 8:32;Philippians 4:19). Jehova-Rophi-*The Lord, The Physician*; (Matthew 12:15;Jeremiah 3:22; 8:22;Psalm 147:3;). Jehovah-Nissi-*The Lord Our Banner*; (Psalm 20:5; 60:4;Exodus 17:15,16;Isaiah 5:26; 49:22; 62:10). Jehovah M'Kaddesh-*The Lord Doth Sanctify*; (Exodus 19:5,6; 31:13; I Corinthians 6:11). Jehovah-Eloheenu-*Lord Our God*; (Psalm 99:5,8,9). Jehovah-Eloheka-*Lord Thy God*; (Deuteronomy 16;Exodus:20:2). Jehovah-Elohay-*The Lord My God*; (Judges 6:15; 13:8;Zechariah 14:5; Psalm 7:1; 18:28; 30:2; 30:12). Jehovah-Shalom-*The Lord Our Peace*; (Genesis 15:15; Judges 6:24; 19:20; I Samuel 25:6). Jehovah-Tsebaoth-*The Lord of Hosts*; (I Samuel 1:3; Jeremiah 11:20; Psalm 46:7; Romans 9:29; James 5:4). Jehovah-Rohi-*The Lord is My Shepherd*; (Psalm 23:1; 6). Jehovah-Tsidkenu-*The Lord Our Righteousness*; (Jeremiah 23:5,6; 33:16; Leviticus 19:35,36). Jehovah-Makkeh-*The Lord Shall Smite Thee*; (Ezekiel 7:9; 22:13;I Peter 4:17;Revelation 2:16;Malachi 4:6). Jehovah-Gmolah-*The God of Recompenses*; (Jeremiah 51:1,7,8; 51:56; Deuteronomy 32:35; Romans 12:17-21). Jehovah-Shammah-*The Lord is There*; (Ezekiel 48:35; Deuteronomy 4:37;Psalm 132:8,13,14).

We read to know that we are not alone.

C.S. Lewis

Chapter One

Your True Identity

In the beginning, it was all about you. You were the sole bene-
ficiary of God's actions. God didn't need the Heavens and the
earth; He created them for you. God didn't need the sun, moon, and
stars; He put them in the sky for you. God didn't need the light - He
was and is the Eternal light; He let there be light for you. God didn't
need a Garden of Eden; He created it as an all-sufficient environment in which you could live.

God made Adam and Eve from the very dust of the earth He
created. He made them perfect - in His image, without sin - and
provided them with everything good. He endowed them with a
unique quality - a free will. This was a supreme act of grace. Now
independent, they had an opportunity to show God their adoration,
love, and trust by their own choosing. Adam and Eve could remain
sinless through obedience or choose evil when it was presented. It
was becoming obvious God loved them, but He didn't need them;
they needed God.

When presented with sin, Adam and Eve chose evil. By their
deliberate choice, they each relinquished the perfection, provision,
and protection that had been theirs prior to sin. Discovering their
sinless nature gone and their true identity lost, they found themselves suddenly misplaced - alienated from God. Their purity and
their identity in God were gone. Now they had to seek a way back to
the creator. How on earth could they reconcile what they had done?

They were driven from the garden, and all humanity that followed inherited their sin. Mankind was destined to have a sinful nature with a propensity to sin.

Recognizing their condition as perilous, God integrated into human beings a knowledge of Himself, so that even in our imperfect state, we might recognize His existence. From Adam and Eve's first trial, God was displaying His grace. He didn't want us to have a reference point of sin only, but also one of hope, forgiveness, and reinstatement. It was in the garden that we saw God's plan of redemption begin.

God wants you to have a true identity in Christ, your own special place in the family of God, your own personal Garden of Eden. This could be called your *garden identity*, which is your persona closest to the perfection of Adam and Eve before sin. Can you ever achieve that past perfection? This side of Heaven, it is impossible. But now you have a choice: either follow God in obedience or deny His existence. One choice leads directly to mercy and forgiveness, and one choice leads to estrangement, sorrow, and pain.

God has a plan for your restoration, a way to regain your true identity. God sent His son - His only begotten son – to die for you. Jesus Christ became flesh and blood and lived among flesh and blood. Jesus came into this world, not only to show us what God is, but to show us what we should be and how we should live. Jesus lived and died to be raised up, to rejoin the Father, and to intercede for you.

The physical universe proves that God has established order in His creation. God has a divine plan for all humanity, so it's reasonable that He should have an orderly plan to carry on His work. From that perspective, it's all about you.

When you hear and believe the Gospel, when you repent and obey God, when you see Jesus Christ as your Lord and Savior, then God sees you without sin. You appear white as snow when God sees you through the shed blood of Christ. The Old Testament prophet Isaiah gives everyone hope with these words, "Come now, let us reason together, says the Lord. Though your sins are like scarlet, they shall be as white as snow; though they are red as crimson, they shall be like wool" (Isaiah 1:18).

These words spoken by God through the prophet Isaiah came with a blessing and a warning. If you are willing and obedient, there is a blessing to come. If you resist and rebel, there is severe punishment forthcoming.

You're an adult and capable of making your own decisions. Do you take the Bible seriously? What has the most influence over you? You encounter many individuals and groups on a daily basis, and each has its own identity and agenda. What you are committed to and passionate about reveals to what and to whom you belong. Who you believe you are drives your thoughts and behavior. You are a home inhabited by your culture, family, friends, and work. God desires to be at the center of your home so your true identity can be realized. By inviting Christ into your home, you manifest God's purpose fulfilled. You will never be the same old self again.

What Jesus said, did, and felt gives us a window into the very heart of the creator. Christ's identification with you changes your relationship with others. Jesus had a direct relationship with His Father and seeks the same with you as your intercessor. Only you can choose to consciously give Jesus authority to enter your home and guide you. Jesus came not only to restore you, but also to free you from the influence and effects of sin. The mysteries of God are slowly being revealed to us through the power of His love and His Holy Spirit.

If you have accepted Jesus Christ as your Lord and Savior, you share in the power of His identity: you will be transformed. You don't have to let the world's expectations rule you. You don't have to feel pressured to be like someone else. You will have a new identity in Christ. When you live, work, and believe the way Jesus lived, worked, and believed, you will have a changed life, a restored life, and a true identity. All of us have the ability to see God at work in our lives, but knowing Him is another matter. That is what God truly desires, that you know Him intimately.

"Philip said, "Lord, show us the Father and that will be
enough for us."
Jesus answered: "Don't you know me, Philip, even after
I have been among you such a long time?
Anyone who has seen me has seen the Father."
John 14:8-9

Jesus always stressed that every word He spoke came from the Father. The closer you come to Jesus, the closer you come to God. Jesus is the ultimate Word of God. Colossians 1:15 tells us that Jesus is the invisible image of God.

What is the most loving action someone has done for you? What is the most loving action you have done for someone else? Your identity is revealed in pure love. God sent Jesus to come and die for you. He rose from the dead for you. He loves you and patiently waits for you. He frees you from invisible chains. Born into a world of pain and joy, suffering from spiritual amnesia, you were a prisoner in your own home. Even so, you were the object of God's love. Jesus has come to redeem you, to make you one with the Father. How can your heart, mind, and actions follow the King of Creation? Jesus is more than the door to heaven; He is the heart of your home.

There are parts of our lives, past and present, that we are ashamed of. They may show us as impure, unclean, illegal, or sinful, but we also know we can turn to God. When we turn to Him, He washes the dirt off our feet so we can walk into His house with strength and purity. God comforts those who journey through tough times while seeking Him. He guides through any storm, any catastrophe, and any heartbreak. Jesus endured this pain and created a path for all to follow. He wants you in heaven. You need His strength to get there. You need His prayers interceding for you.

Prayer is a dynamic process. It is an active dialogue between the potter and the clay. Ask God for help, ask Him for answers, ask Him for comfort. He can answer the difficult questions and help you make wise decisions. If you reach toward God, He will call you to evolve beyond your circumstances. Jesus conquered sin and God wants you to do the same. He desires you to live in harmony and union with Him and His creation.

Life can be hard. The Bible trains you to get through painful trials. God uses these ordeals to strengthen you. Through the living Word, you will discover armies of strength you didn't know you had. This strength is yours and the Lord calls you to cultivate it, to travel through various trials holding tightly to it. Joining together with God, you become a cocreator of a whole new identity. God will give you a place of rest if you travel that narrow path by grace through faith.

> "For it is by grace you have been saved,
> through faith – and this not from yourselves,
> it is the gift of God – not by works,
> so that no one can boast."
> Ephesians 2:8-9

God's glory is the revelation of Jesus' character and presence in you. The lives of Jesus' disciples reveal His character, and He is presented to the world through them. Sinners enter the banquet of God by following His son. When we accept Jesus into our hearts, the Holy Spirit becomes ours, and we become members of the body of Christ. Just as Jesus entered our world, He asks us to enter His. Jesus extends the invitation, but ultimately it is you who must respond in faith.

You were given special skills and God will help them grow in you. Jesus practiced strengths the Heavenly Father gave him; strengths to heal the sick, feed the hungry, teach Scripture, raise the dead, and talk to God – because of who He was. God did not do this *for* Him; instead, He gave Jesus the power and choice to practice His talents. Jesus maximized His gifts, using them to open the doors of Heaven. God will help you maximize your gifts as you come closer to Jesus. The abilities and talents you use help shape your destiny. If you cultivate your talents and strengths, God will reveal His glory in you, and He will open the doors of Heaven to others through you.

God gave you multiple gifts to use - some obvious, some hidden. Thank Him for all you are. Thank Him for your family and friends. Thank Him for your health, your job, your church, and your free will - for your very life. Thank Him for everything present and future.

Thank Him for revealing Himself to you through the Bible. He loves you unconditionally. Go to Jesus with your prayers and questions. Ask for understanding and for strength to follow Him. Rely on Him, and patiently wait for His answers. Put your whole essence into your prayers. He will guide you to understand His transformational powers.

> "Trust in the Lord with all your heart and lean not on
> your own understanding; in all your ways acknowledge
> him, and he will make your paths straight."
> Proverbs 3:5-6

Leaning means putting your whole weight on some *thing* or some *one* else, trusting in them to support you. When you have an important decision to make and feel alone, like you can't trust anyone, trust God. He wants to lead, guide, and direct you. He wants to protect you, and dialogue with you. He is the best judge of what you need. Trust Him, listen to Him, and go to your Bible for guidance. He will show you a straight path. He wants you to make Him a vital part of everything you do and are. He eagerly desires to be invited into your home. Is Christ presently standing at the door of your home, knocking, waiting patiently to be let in? Do you hear Him? Are you even listening?

As you live closer to the Lord, you will see how much He loves you. You will find that every action and thought has a consequence related to how you experience God. You will realize that the Lord has helped you with every trial. You can decide to let the Spirit shape you, while enduring the storm's worst. Deep down, you know that God sees everything you do. What kind of path do you wish to have walked when you stand before your maker and explain your life's choices?

Make life choices that bring you closer to God's love. Study God's word so that He can continue to strengthen your talents. Focus on His spiritual commands, not your desires. Pray with people, tell others about your God, and invest yourself in a church where you can learn and help others. Everyone runs in the race of life. Run your race to win others for the cause of Christ.

The paths to heaven and hell are two different journeys. It takes a commitment and a rebirth to see the polarizing horizons. This world and everything in it will one day pass away. Follow the crumbs of heaven, where a banquet awaits. God is calling and wants you to return home.

> "Show me your ways, O Lord, teach me your paths;
> guide me in your truth and teach me,
> for you are God my Savior,
> and my hope is in you all day long."
> Psalms 25:4-5

Love is one of God's greatest gifts. You were created with love, to be loved. You were created with a basic need for love and an instinct to love. You were created to love others. But first and foremost, you were created to love your God.

> "Teacher, which is the greatest commandment in the Law?"
> Jesus replied: "'Love the Lord your God with all your heart
> and with all your soul and with all your mind.'
> This is the first and greatest commandment."
> Matthew 22:36-38

God's love is unconditional, everlasting, immutable, and perfect. God's love is the only love that will never fail. You're commanded to love God with everything you are because God is your loving creator and your only hope. He wants you to realize your true identity in Christ and become a new creation in heaven.

God's desire is for you to come to Him. Knowing Him is like no other relationship you have ever had; it must be sincere, heartfelt, and genuine. You reach out for His love, seek it, desire it, accept it, and He will respond. His faithfulness is great. His mercies are new every morning. All you need, He can provide. God is in you, with you, and beside you – always.

One day, you are going to answer to God. Your life lived is your response. Our choices in life will matter far beyond the consequences of their effect here. God judges us, and He is just. We struggle to understand what that means, but you can be certain about one thing: after your final breath, when you are before Christ, then you will realize that it's going to be *all about you*!

Chapter Two

Seeking Reconciliation

In the relentless march toward civilization mankind has made great strides. People are living longer; diseases once feared can now be treated, even cured. Transportation, science, industry, and even food have been transformed from necessities to luxuries. There are hybrid cars, wireless telephones, televisions that bring the entire world into our homes, and global satellites in space that can track your every move – anywhere in the world! There are computers that talk, ovens that cook without heat, machines that can find fish under water, and a church on every corner. A modern world can be a wonderful place. If the ancients could return, what would they say?

After being amazed and amused for a spell, they would look over all the changes, shake their wise old heads and say, "Some things will never change." In all their wisdom, they would tell us, "Despite all your progress, man still needs God as much as ever." And they would be exactly right in any time or in any culture.

The future is not something to be feared. In the Old Testament the prophet Daniel saw glimpses of future kingdoms and beyond. Some parts he understood, and some events God told him to just *write it down* so that others following him would understand it. Daniel was given a prophecy that was to be sealed and kept secret. Its purpose was to let people living in the end times, you and me, know that God sees the future and the role we will play in it.

"But thou, O Daniel, shut up the words,
and seal the book, even to the time of the end:
many shall run to and fro,
and knowledge shall be increased."
Daniel 12:4 KJV

In the Garden of Eden, when Adam and Eve made aprons of fig leaves to cover themselves, something happened; they had dangerously decided to improve themselves without God. But their new clothing was inadequate – they were still naked. Their hiding place was inadequate – they could not elude God. Their excuses were inadequate – they were still guilty. They had started down a road beyond the garden that all their descendants would have to follow.

Adam and Eve got a glimpse of the future and it wasn't as appealing as their garden home. God seemed afar off and their identity changed. They had to seek a way to reconcile with their creator, but the role of reconciliation wasn't going to be their responsibility.

Reconciliation simply means reestablishing a relationship. There are numerous reasons a relationship fractures, but the root cause is always sin. We cannot seek reconciliation on our own terms. Although it's well-intentioned, we have the temerity to inform God that somehow, by our works, we can make the relationship right again. Simply put, only Christ is the remedy for our alienation from God.

Reconcile means not only to change, but also to change thoroughly. For something this challenging, we need help beyond ourselves. Only Christ can reconcile us to God and to each other, because reconciliation is the work of God alone; man has no part.

We are blissfully ignorant and content until the Lord God comes walking into our Garden of Eden. We can't hide; our world is too small. We hang our heads and sink into the quicksand of guilt and shame. Conviction never reaches our soul until God asks, "Where are you?"

Paralyzed with fear, we desire to hide from God instead of seeking Him out. Our circumstances have changed. Our halo of innocence has fled along with our identity. While we attempt to find our place, sin swirls around us like smoke from a fire. Without your feeling it, sin attaches its tentacles around you and pulls you closer to the embers. You're definitely not in the garden anymore. You're uncomfortable and you're searching for some safe place. You don't desire this fallen environment. You're looking for a way back to God; you're seeking reconciliation. "Therefore, if anyone is in Christ, he is a new creation; the old has gone, the new has come! All this is from God, who reconciled us to himself through Christ" (2 Corinthians 5:17-18).

It was only by the death of Christ that the relationship between God and the world was changed. There is a reconciliation brought about by God in the sinner, where the sinner becomes changed in his attitude toward God. This change persuades him to receive the reconciliation already accomplished by Christ at the cross (see Romans 5:11).

Reconciliation gives us a changed relationship with God because our trespasses and sins are not counted against us. Currently the nation of Israel has rejected Jesus as the true Messiah. This decision has caused the nation to lose favor with God. Although this rejection has lasted for two thousand years, it is temporary. When the Lord returns, the Jewish people will be regathered, rejudged, restored, redeemed, and reconciled to God. Eventually everything will be brought into unity in God, even if judgment is involved (see 1 Corinthians 15:24-28). The old departs, the new arrives.

If we're comfortable in the world, we've already been blinded. This world is not our home. Do you really want to settle for this stop in the road, when Jesus said He was going to prepare a place for us so that we could also be where He is (see John 14:2). If this is not your goal, you are settling for much less than God promised.

If you are a Christian, you are Christ's signature. You are His perfume, His aroma. The world knows Him by knowing you. Clean yourself up, stand upright, live a life of gratitude and service. You are an ambassador, a son, and an heir.

In the Old Testament, Abraham was a patriarch. The Bible calls him a friend of God. When God called Abraham from the land of Ur and instructed him to move to a new country, sight unseen, Abraham packed up and moved. Being obedient, he moved to an unknown location, trusting in God's providential care. And God provided.

After many weeks of travel, to Abraham's amazement, God appeared to him at Bethel. Humbled, it was there Abraham built an altar to God.

Bethel, meaning *House of God*, provided Abraham with the peace he was longing for. It was here that Abraham walked and talked with God. Bethel was Abraham's Garden of Eden. It was here Abraham was finding his true identity. Reconciliation was shadowing Abraham's steps. Life was full and purposeful and obedience to God was fulfilling. For reasons we do not know, Abraham packed up and continued moving farther south. His sense of comfort and belonging slowly faded as Bethel became more distant.

Without direction, Abraham moved away from the place of blessing. Each day's travel took him closer to Egypt. Then there was a famine in the land. It was here Abraham made his second mistake; he descended into Egypt.

While wandering in Egypt, Abraham found no comfort or joy as he had at Bethel. At the altar, he found sustenance and fellowship in God's presence. In Egypt, he had no contact with God and his misery grew daily. His planning and scheming overshadowed God. His peace was replaced with anxiety and worry. He nearly lost his life!

Abraham reasoned that this was no different from Ur. God wanted Abraham to draw near to Him, not wander aimlessly. There was but one thing to do: return to the place where grace lived, where the presence of God lingered. He was compelled to return to his Eden, where his true identity came alive. He had to seek God's presence. He had to return to Bethel.

What would you have done? Return to Bethel, stay put, go farther into Egypt? Abraham saw his situation deteriorate and decided to return to where God's presence resided. At this point in Abraham's life, where sight gave way to faith, the whisper of reconciliation was calling. God had promised and delivered, but Abraham was not satisfied. Abraham *heard* God at Ur, but he *found* God at Bethel.

The unknown can be turned over to God. Exercise your faith; you will find God is not so far away. You may have sensed God's presence but wandered into a fog of uncertainty. Retrace your steps; remember when God was close. There is a way back to God. A way back to Bethel. You know it, but you must act upon it. The promises God makes to you, He keeps.

"The Lord is not slow in keeping His promise,
as some understand slowness.
He is patient with you, not wanting anyone to perish,
but everyone to come to repentance."
2 Peter 3:9

Almost everyone remembers the story of Samson and Delilah. Samson was one of God's anointed who walked with God but also wandered into iniquity. He was no ordinary man: a judge over Israel, a Nazarene, and the world's strongest man! Samson was dedicated at birth to God. His life was reserved for greatness. His purpose was to begin delivering the nation of Israel out of the Philistines' control.

Sent to rout the Philistines, Samson instead was fatally attracted to a Philistine woman. Her beauty pulled him to the flame of disobedience. His heart of faith was drawn to God, but his sensual self was drawn to Delilah. His thoughts and his actions were at war.

Given enormous strength to showcase God's power and abilities, Samson used his gifts most foolishly. Warned repeatedly of his sweetheart's treachery, he simply couldn't, or wouldn't, stay away. Neither could he outwit the wily daughter of his enemies.

Upon learning the secret of his strength, Samson's enemies, who were also God's enemies, captured him. The Philistines' chief nemesis, this proudly religious Nazarite, was finally taken prisoner, blinded, and put into the enemy's dungeon. The mighty Samson, once Israel's pride, now found himself reduced to grinding grain like an ox in the yoke.

When Samson was brought out of prison and put on display like a circus act, the Philistines boasted of their prized catch, all to the humiliation of their enemy, Israel. Samson knew that he was moved from prison to the great Temple of Dagon, the Philistine god, for further humiliation. His heart ached for God to hear one final prayer, a prayer of reconciliation. Asking for great strength once more, Samson prayed for the ability to push apart the supporting pillars and wreck the Temple of Dagon. Quietly, God heard and granted Samson's request. The pillars yielded and the great roof collapsed, killing thousands, including Samson.

Samson was never so weak as when he was too proud of his strength. He failed to see that God's presence alone does not overtake a person's will. Enticed by Delilah, Samson's decisions caused disobedience and resulted in untold heartache. Did Samson remember Delilah while alone in prison? Would you remember the woman who betrayed your deepest secret or would you remember the faithfulness of God?

God never forgot or abandoned Samson. God never forgets or abandons you. Samson's final act of obedience turned God's ear. God restored him and answered his prayer. In spite of your past, God still loves you. The terrible consequences of sin remain, but God's grace abounds even more. God is seeking a sign of repentance, He is seeking a prayer of confession, and He is seeking reconciliation with you.

Our lives are roadmapped for service. Any detours that lead us away from God's will are self-determined. God will help steer our life back on course for His purposes. Only we ourselves stand in the way of being used by God as planned. Be obedient to His Word, be submissive to His callings, and be reconciled to His family.

Away from God's Spirit for years, Samson was reunited with God for one moment, with one prayer. God turned Samson's failures into victory. For you and for me, it is never too late to seek God and start over. In the New Testament, Hebrews 11 records the stories of Abraham and Samson and others who, by faith, subdued kingdoms, wrought righteousness, obtained promises, and were made strong. You too can be counted with Abraham and Samson. God's grace extends across the centuries. You need reconciliation now more than ever.

There is no excuse for remaining unreconciled to God. He has approached you with love through His son Jesus Christ. He has done all He can do; now – it's all about you and your response.

Chapter Three

Walking on Water

In the Gospel of John, Jesus said, "In this world you *will* have trouble" (John 16:33, emphasis added). Jesus did not say you *might* have trouble. Everyone reading these words knows this is true. Trouble is spread over the whole world because sin contaminated the earth and everything on it. Some of our inevitable troubles are small puddles; some are puddles, but seem to us like oceans; and some really are big turbulent oceans. How do we differentiate between what is minor, simply upsetting, or critical?

First, you must realize that no matter what, no situation is too big for God. A seasoned minister recently said, "How we see the problem *is* the problem". What do you think he meant by that? As another put it, "Don't focus on how big your problem is, but how big your God is!" God is bigger than whatever problem you encounter. Jesus said, "...all things are possible with God" (Mark 10:27). Do you believe that? When a crisis arrives, will you believe that?

We need to distinguish between ripples on the water's surface and towering waves that create havoc. Why does the house always need repairs, why isn't my job secure, and why isn't there ever enough money? The test results came back from the doctor, it looks like surgery is necessary and the insurance may not protect me. Why did cancer slowly overtake my friend, leaving behind a single parent with three small children and crushing debt? Puddles versus oceans.

The Bible gives us an excellent example of someone going through heart-wrenching troubles and shows us what was learned from it all. The story also shows us what *we* can learn from this experience with God.

One day Satan approached the throne of God and they had a conversation. God said to Satan, "Have you considered my servant Job?...he is blameless and upright, a man who fears God..." (see Job 1:8). Satan accused God of protecting Job, saying, "But stretch out your hand and strike everything he has, and he will surely curse you to your face" (Job 1:11).

God agreed to the test, but set limits on Satan by saying, "Everything he has is in your hands, but on the man himself do not lay a finger" (Job 1:12). Satan's first attack was on Job's possessions. Thinking he was selfish and materialistic, Satan struck where he thought Job was weakest. With God's permission, the assault on Job began. Unknown to Job, his life was about to be tested to the outer limits.

The first attack came in the space of one day. Within hours, everything Job had was destroyed, taken captive, or killed. This included seven thousand sheep, three thousand camels, five hundred yoke of oxen, five hundred donkeys, and sadly, his family of ten grown children! Only Job, his wife, and a few servants survived the calamities. In a matter of hours, Satan had struck and destroyed a lifetime of work. Then Satan waited for Job's reply to this catastrophe. Crushed but not defeated, Job did not sin by blaming God. He humbled himself to his Sovereign.

> "Naked came I out of my mother's womb,
> and naked shall I return."
> Job 1:21 KJV

Job had endured a plethora of staggering losses in his life in a matter of hours, and yet none of these epic troubles were of his own making. Even though he couldn't understand why this was happening, he knew it wasn't because of any sin he committed. He maintained his innocence, but there was more trouble to come.

Soon after this happened Satan launched a second attack, this time on Job himself. While God cannot be goaded into doing anything outside His divine purpose, Satan was allowed to afflict Job with painful sores. Again, God limited Satan's power – he could not take Job's life. Job was in agony but he still maintained his innocence, and laid the blame on no one.

Job's condition should be examined a little further to see the lengths to which Satan pushed this righteous man. The skin covering his entire body was affected, from the soles of his feet to the top of his head. He itched intensely (see Job 2:8) and was in acute pain (see v.13). His flesh became hard and crusty and attracted worms (see Job 7:5); it seeped with a serum that turned dark in color (see Job 7:5; 30:30). He had a fever and constantly aching bones (see Job 30:17,30), nightmares (see Job 7:14), and extreme weight loss (see Job 17:7, 19:20).

Can you just picture the poor man in agony? Do you feel any of his pain? There was more! Job was ill, but his sickness caused him to be "unclean" and socially unacceptable. He used a piece of broken pottery to scrape his sores to get some relief. More sores appeared. We don't know exactly what his afflictions were, just the gruesome symptoms. The issue is not the disease, but Job's attitude in his response. His wife suggested that he should just curse God and die. But Job replied, "Shall we accept good from God, and not trouble?" (Job 2:10).

When Job's friends heard of his troubles, they came to sympathize with him and comfort him. They came to grieve with him over his losses and his broken health. When they first saw him they barely recognized him. They wept for him and with him. For one full week they sat with Job in silence, then they gently began to analyze why trouble happens to people and more specifically, to him. You are not alone when you ask, why me? Where is God when I need help? But there was still more to come.

After months of dialogue, his friends concluded that Job's great suffering was the result of some sin Job had committed and this was God's punishment. Although Job reacted with some hostility, he maintained his innocence. He always turned back to God. He never renounced God. Like Job's friends, we think we have all the answers. Job's friends were all very logical in their approach, but they were all very wrong!

Job's greatest trial was not the suffering, but not understanding *why* he was suffering. Job questioned God and asked for answers. Job knew it wasn't because of sin, but for a time God was silent on the matter. It's critical to remember that in the worst of suffering, Job trusted God completely. The problem is without solution, but not without understanding. We understand that some things are under God's purview and that is sufficient.

God's ways are not our ways. They are beyond our comprehension. We shouldn't expect or demand that God explain everything. We wouldn't need faith and trust if we had all the answers to life's problems. God understands our concerns and questions. God is in complete and absolute control. God loves us unconditionally, and that's enough.

Troubles are always imminent, they continually settle on our lives like accumulating dust. Do nothing and they bury us. Some perturbances are self-inflicted and some are thrust upon us unaware. Often they can seem more powerful than you. God does not ignore your circumstances, wants, and needs. You might not get quick and easy answers to your prayers, but God promises that He will go with you through your trials and tribulations. The rigors of hardship can be useful; they inspire us to approach God in new ways. Know this - God is bigger than our understanding of Him. His love for us is more than our love for Him.

Troubles weave in and out of your life. Do not be shocked or surprised when they arrive uninvited, they are inevitable. Once dilemmas visit, then what? Determine whether they are puddles or oceans then adjust your response accordingly. God permits difficulties to enter our lives for a reason. Sometimes this is to test our character, or teach us a life lesson, or to exercise our patience. God may be using a particular trial to draw you closer to Him. When afflictions come, great or small, how do you give them over to God?

Uncertainty and danger have the effect of sharply focusing our priorities regarding survival. You know that we live in an uncertain world that is becoming more precarious. You also know that this world is a dangerous place. Anything could happen tragically and unexpectedly. The major television networks, cable news, the Internet, even newspaper headlines, all lend uneasiness to our daily routine. And when disturbances come, God waits for our response.

God desires that we seek Him first. Why? Because living our lives without God's help leads to confusion, anguish, and ultimately, defeat. God should be the first place we turn when facing any dilemma or struggle. Staying in daily contact with God lessens our painful circumstances. Be thankful for problems and troubles; they put us in a position to watch God work in our lives.

Small problems require small answers, but giant problems permit God to show us His awesome power. On the Sea of Galilee during a violent storm, the apostles screamed for help, but Christ spoke the storm out of existence. God spoke you into existence; He can speak you into a new existence. God won't avoid your problems; He often works when you least expect it. There is no problem too complicated for God. Don't deny God the pleasure of helping you in times of need.

Some issues are difficult to release to God. Our situation becomes worse when our problems are the result of flirting with sin. We want the discomfort removed, but our pride wants to remain in control. There is danger in solving problems in our own way. Our situation becomes bearable if we turn to God when our challenges first arise. God does not want us to focus on our weakness, but on His strength, His words, and on His ability.

See your troubles for what they are - a growing experience. You make a conscious decision to release your anxiety to God, trusting Him to handle it without your assistance. Just saying we believe God can handle our problems isn't enough. We need to act on it by choosing to release them, trusting Him to deal with it, and praying that our will is folded into His will. Then live as though you believe God can do what He says. Jesus reminded the disciples about the power of prayer, "Ask and it will be given to you; seek and you will find; knock and the door will be opened to you" (Matthew 7:7).

The minutiae and cares of this world can choke the joy out of us if we permit it. Troubles and such will be with us for only a lifetime, but God will be around forever and ever. We should lay aside our cares and endeavor to know our creator and sustainer. Learn about

Jesus; come to know God. Learn about God; find your purpose, your passion, and your duty.

God works in *all* things, not just isolated incidents. He is woven into the fabric of your daily life. He is the world's heartbeat. When you ask for guidance, you acknowledge His ability and your disability. The hardships that visit you beg for God's attention. Determine to trust God and let your understanding grow as a result.

Most problems or decisions are multidimensional. When the area of decision-making exceeds our realm of knowledge, there must be a belief or a hope to replace the lack of knowledge. This is where faith becomes incarnate.

You yearn for peace, beauty, and happiness because you ultimately yearn for heaven. You are created to bond with your Creator, but the choice to seek Him is yours, and yours alone. Problems want to separate you from God, but God calls you to trust Him. You are invited to sit at the table with Him.

God can turn your circumstances around. Your faith is stronger than any calamity. Do you understand that God is not working to make you happy, but fulfilled? God's ultimate desire is to see us become more Christlike. The more we become like Him, the closer we come to reaching our true identity. God calls you to have faith.

Many people love sin; they are governed by unconscious patterns of thinking and behavior until their sin overtakes them. The Bible says men love darkness more than light. We are living in a world of powerful unseen forces. But God's love is the most powerful force in creation. Our faith and hope in God make us stronger than any storm. Our interpretation of God is often flawed and shortsighted, but His interpretation of us is true. He loves us and wants us to have freedom in Him and through Him.

We have a role and a responsibility to effect a change in ourselves with God's help. The tools to make this change are not simple works that we must do, but an attitude of submission and obedience to God's will. This is to be a joint effort; we must cooperate with God, because our efforts alone will not suffice.

Troubles are disguised in various shapes and visit us intermittently. Instead of asking, "Why me, Lord?", consider asking, "What are you trying to show or teach me?" Trials can be caused by sin or a lack of faith. Trials can also be a direct part of God's plan for your life. Hardship builds character, develops patience, and makes us sensitive to others' suffering. The book of Ecclesiastes says the rain falls on the just and the unjust! No one is immune to troubles. Moses, Job, Saint Peter - they all had their share of difficulties. Should we be exempt because we live in a different age?

God walked *on* the water; we must walk *through* it. Sometimes God parts the waters as He did for Moses; other times, He guides us through it if we have faith and hold firmly to His hand. God will ask you to be a helping hand that helps raise up others. You are asked to be a shepherd and a servant. Jesus reached out to people. He asks that you reach out a hand to help others. What can you do? What can you hope to offer someone else?

You have already conquered storms. Use your life experience to witness to those in need. Share your faith and what God has done in your life. Look for an opportunity to help another. God has made an abundance of opportunities for you to share with Him and others. Because God has helped us with our problems, we can comfort others. Life is brief and our days are numbered; make every day and every opportunity count. Use what you've learned to help others. Your experience can be their light. Give them hope. Give them a cup of water in Jesus' name. Be amazing to God.

Are there poor people in your community? Volunteer in a homeless shelter. Visit a nursing home, mentor a child, find someone who feels neglected or lonely and comfort him. These people are important to God. He will help you build a relationship. Jesus asks that you share your time, your abilities, and your faith, because "And we know that in all things God works for the good of those who love Him, who have been called according to his purpose" (Romans 8:28).

Not everything that happens to us is good. There is evil in this fallen world, but God can turn it into good. Trust in God, not in things that will fade with time. Learn to accept troubles, because God can be found in them. When Jesus was hanging on that Roman cross, He was a light pinned against the darkness, but He was not alone. God was with Christ when the nails were driven into His wrists, and He will be with you when unbearable hardships come. When you are caught in a big turbulent ocean, let God reign.

The life of Job is a heartbreaking drama. It is a treatise about pain and suffering and divine sovereignty. But more than that, it's a picture of faith and trust in the light of terrible suffering. Satan, who accused Job of being deceitful, is proven deceitful himself when he tries to discredit the Lord through Job (see Job 2:3). Job's losses were devastating, but in the end God gave Job twice the amount of livestock Satan took from him. He had ten more children in addition to the ten that had gone to heaven. Everything Job previously had was doubled!

Although God finally responded to Job, He questioned Job in the same way Job had questioned Him. He gave him no answers, no reasons. God doesn't have to explain Himself to man. However, God did not declare Job's innocence or guilt. Job's faith was strengthened by his suffering. He realized he had spoken more from ignorance than from understanding, and that he had only heard of God before his ordeal, and now he had *seen* God. God continued to refer to him as "my servant Job", the same way He described him to Satan.

Job had his troubles; you will have your troubles. Job's friends helped him try to understand his dilemma; your friends may do the same. When all your options are exhausted, and all your questions are still unanswered, listen for the voice of God, and be thankful that God is still there after all. Learn some lessons from Job's life, because the next time Satan inquires of God, it may be all about you!

Chapter Four

Letter from Paradise

The Bible is humanity's greatest asset and sadly the one irreplaceable treasure most people take for granted. Ever since Moses came down from Mount Sinai with the Ten Commandments, the whole world has known what God expected from the human race. From the Old Testament leather and papyrus scrolls on which Moses wrote, to the completed New Testament finished in 95 A.D. by John the Apostle, God has tried repeatedly to be a part of our lives. The Bible is a historical road map with Christ serving as our compass to secure our destination. He will lead us beside the still waters, through green pastures, through the valley of the shadow of death, right into the House of the Lord - the place of ultimate freedom we're all seeking.

Reading the Bible is an adventure that is immensely transforming. It is a journey across a cosmic abyss. The Bible is your passport to understanding God's mysteries and our role in His creation. God created within us an innate knowledge of His existence, but we have to use the resources at our disposal to seek, find, and know Him. Although one can glean a basic understanding from an experience, a friend, or a church, the Bible is our primary resource for intimately knowing our Creator. The writing is inspired and essential to our daily lives. The Bible is a priceless possession, it is a ticket to reconciliation, it is a letter from paradise.

Can we trust the Bible, this letter from paradise? It helps to know that it has withstood the test of time. For over two thousand years it has guided nations, given rulers wisdom, offered hope to the poor and downtrodden, and been the seed of anything good that has come out of this sin-soaked world. God said, "Heaven and earth will pass away, but my words will never pass away" (Matthew 24:35). That doesn't just include "within your lifetime", it includes "within time itself"!

"All Scripture is God-breathed and is useful for teaching,
rebuking, correcting and training in righteousness,
so that the man of God may be thoroughly equipped
for every good work."
2 Timothy 3:16-17

All Scripture is God-breathed and trustworthy because God was in control of its writing. The Bible is authoritative for our lives and our faith. God's Spirit is our tutor for the Bible. The Bible shows us who we are and who He is. It is our only way of knowing how we can be saved. As you come closer to God, you begin to let Him live in and through you. You start to live in the world through a Christ-consciousness.

The message of the Bible reveals that God wants to have an intimate relationship with you. He wants to raise you above life's destructive paths. Jesus lived this message for thirty-three years so it could serve as our example. Ever since His resurrection, God's means and ends of reaching you were – and are – Love. He died for you because He loves you. He rose from the grave because He loves you. He gave you the Bible because He loves you. Reason with Him for a moment. Is not life more powerful than death, love more powerful than hate, and God more powerful than sin?

He did not create you to abandon you, entirely the opposite. He wants to dialogue with you. If you feel lost, seek God, for He is seeking you. He gave you a mind, a heart, and a will to communicate with Him. How do you use these gifts? By drawing close to Him, and joining in the celebration He offers.

By showing the world His eternal power and divine nature, God made Himself known to all. By rejecting God's authority and position, the world indicts itself. We hide from our creator, yet the creator seeks us out. Through sin, we have removed ourselves from Him, but God desires to remove the sin and restore the sinner. His Word serves as the blueprint for this restoration. Even though we rebel, He forgives. What an act of grace on His part! Would you be so generous and considerate?

In the Old Testament book of Isaiah, God said, "For my thoughts are not your thoughts, neither are your ways my ways, declares the Lord. As the heavens are higher than the earth, so are my ways higher than your ways and my thoughts than your thoughts" (Isaiah 55:8-9). They are nobler, purer, and more Holy. It is impossible to know or understand God unless He communicates to us through His Word. His words transform us; they guide our mind, affect our feelings, and direct our actions. Words mean different things to different people, but God's words bring us all closer to Him. They are the words to eternal life. His words are infallible, inspired, and indestructible.

The construction of the Bible is unlike any other book. It is a compilation of sixty-six different books written by over thirty-three separate authors from various backgrounds, spanning several continents over a period of fifteen hundred years. And yet miraculously it has a consistent, rhythmic, harmonious theme: a coming Messiah portrayed as a sacrificial lamb for the sins of the world, a kinsman redeemer for all mankind. A lamb without spot or blemish to provide reconciliation to us, so a fallen creation can assume its proper place in paradise.

God guided the pen strokes of each author and they became coauthors with God, led by His Spirit. The Bible has a unity of thought showing that one mind orchestrated both the compilation and the writing. God Himself superintended and directed the human writers to create a work of divine origin through human means. God gave us the Bible so we could understand Him.

There is a persistent theme in the Old Testament showing that the God of the Hebrew nation will become the God of all nations. It is history, poetry, and prophecy; yet within all the various parts, there is a harmony of the whole. Thank God that He has preserved and protected it down through the centuries for our benefit.

The words of God will stand on their own. His word realized in you will be your happiness. God's words, written for you, are holy, binding, and everlasting. The Bible has an impressive ability to endure through any test or trial.

It's important to note what's not in the Bible. It is not a record of man's effort to find God. It is an account of God's effort to reveal Himself to mankind. It is not a record of the human race becoming better. It is an account of man's nature to lie, murder, steal, kill, and invent other gods to worship. It is not a record of man's goodness and accomplishments. It is an accounting of the Creator offering forgiveness, reconciliation, and a home in paradise for eternity.

The Bible is enduring, firm, and permanent. It was originally written on perishable material called papyrus. But it has survived. Written on scrolls before the printing press, it was penned by hand, meticulously, without error. But it has survived. During the early years of the church, the Romans burned every copy of the Scriptures they could confiscate. They tried to destroy the seed of Christianity. But it has survived. The Bible is *still* flourishing; are the Romans?

Scholars have split hairs and denominations over the books of the Bible. Who wrote what, and when, are always topics of debate that waste valuable time and resources. Historical criticism and textual criticism are tests of authenticity and originality. Both are necessary and prudent in determining the Scripture's purity and divinity. We need to face the obvious: after nineteen centuries, the Bible has stood the test of time and excelled as the absolute standard of truth and divine intervention.

Translations from Hebrew to Greek to Latin to English all have one thing in common: the truth remains. The message of God's love is undiluted. Christ's death, burial, and resurrection are undisputed. Prophecy is still being fulfilled, and the second coming of Christ is closer than ever. Rather than arguing over whether a comma was misplaced by a medieval scribe, shouldn't we be trusting God for the Bible's accuracy? The Bible is His word; can't we trust the creator of the universe to keep His letter from paradise pure and unadulterated? If you believe in the One who inspired the Bible, why not believe He maintained the purity of the Bible?

The Dead Sea Scrolls proved without doubt the accuracy of the text of the Old Testament. With thousands of manuscripts of the New Testament in existence today, it is the most authentic document of all ancient writings. God has preserved, protected, and produced the most reliable and accurate account of His word – all for you!

Although it has been analyzed, criticized, and ridiculed, it perseveres because it is enduring, trustworthy, and has deep heavenly roots. You can discard it, defame it, or deny it, but the Bible will always represent the truth and be the means of salvation for countless millions.

God wants you to know the truth. Jesus himself is the Truth. He is the source and essence of truth personified. Jesus taught His disciples the words of truth with love. But beware: Satan uses deception to turn you away from the truth. Take heart, for Jesus gave us some of the most comforting words in the whole Bible when He said, "I am the way and the truth and the life. No one comes to the Father except through me" (John 14:6).

Everyone needs to read the Bible. It is the Word of God and it speaks for Him. It contains the most beautiful story ever told. It gives life meaning, joy, purpose, hope, and victory. In it are the words by which to live our lives. There is nothing to compare it to in all the world. Nothing! It is a personal love letter from paradise to all the lost souls on this earth.

The Bible is a book filled with signs, but it is also a book of wonders:

- It speaks to you personally
- Its message is unified throughout
- Its accuracy is preserved and proven
- Its influence is seen all over the world
- Its subject matter is consistent and relevant
- It has the capacity to change the human heart
- It has the ability to penetrate to your soul and spirit

There are worlds of complex thought in the Bible, but even a child can understand most of its messages. Biblical scholars study writing styles, linguistics, prophecy, and cultural shifts. But even you can study its historical significance, how it influences individuals, and how the books of history, poetry, and prophecy all conjoin to tell God's great story. Everything we need to know about God is around us, within us, and contained in *The Good Book*.

No other book inspires people to study in groups, to analyze line by line and word by word. God has given you doors of understanding and enlightenment to walk through with His word. Are you interested enough? Are you willing?

How much time do you spend reading God's word? The Bible equips us to do good and to know good from evil. We study the Bible so that we will know Christ, and how to do Christ's work. Knowledge is not useful unless it strengthens our faith and transforms us to live Christlike lives.

We don't need more intelligent arguments. There is sufficient evidence for the Bible's validity. It doesn't matter how smart you are. Intelligence is the ability to gain knowledge and understanding and then apply it to different situations in our life. The problem is not with intelligence, it is one of belief and faith. Jesus said unless you humble yourself and become like a little child, you cannot enter the Kingdom of God (see Matthew 18:3).

God said the Bible *will* accomplish its purpose. It *will* convict us of sin and reveal the deity of Jesus Christ. It *will* motivate us to repent and be obedient to the Lord's commands. It *will* change us from selfishness to service and prepare us for the new heaven and the new earth that are coming.

> "I am God, and there is no other;
> I am God, and there is none like me.
> I make known the end from the beginning,
> from ancient times, what is still to come.
> What I have said, that will I bring about;
> what I have planned, that will I do."
> Isaiah 46: 9-11

The Bible is the most popular and sought-after book ever printed. Having survived and thrived for over nineteen centuries, there are billions of Bibles in circulation. God knew the need would be great, so He greatly multiplied access to His word.

How smart are you? Do you believe the Bible? Have you read *your* letter from paradise? It all starts with you.

Chapter Five

Presence of Evil

We should read the Bible because it enriches our lives, prepares us to live a life pleasing to God, and reinforces us against temptation. The Bible gives us hope, joy, peace, and a hedge of protection against sin. Even though you are made in God's image, sin tries to dominate your life. We live with it and we die with it. Don't give up hope: it's only a part of the world, it's not the world itself.

Sin is subtle, smart, and shrewd. It is an insidious contagion that breeds itself. Sin wants you to be blind to its existence as it spreads through you. It wants to pull you from the mountain, drag you into a pit, and feed on you. Sin is God's enemy and a cancer on all human life. It's a part of your cosmological, biological, and physiological history. You would be wise not to ignore it, because a presence of evil permeates our world.

Evil is the great destroyer that entered the Garden of Eden to take possession of the serpent. Deceiving Adam and Eve, sin gently ushered chaos into the world. Free from sin, we would be totally different creatures. The good news is you have a Savior who conquered sin and death and gives you the eyes to recognize who He is.

God created Adam and Eve to live in the Garden of Eden, tend the garden, be obedient, and live happily ever after. They had no fear of wild animals, and the animals had no fear of them. There was no danger from storms, lightning, earthquakes, floods, or famines. The whole earth was at peace. Adam and Eve had no fear of God, only love for Him. The Genesis 3 account of Adam and Eve's encounter with the serpent might have happened this way:

One day a handsome and plausible stranger walked softly into their peaceful abode. The stranger smiled at Eve and with a voice that was polite and interested asked, "Is it true," he inquired impudently, "you are not allowed to eat the fruit of these trees?"

Eve must have been amused by such a question. "That's not true," she said, "we can eat anything we choose, but we are forbidden to eat the fruit of the Tree of the Knowledge of Good and Evil …or to touch it…or we will die." She told the stranger to do so would be an act of disobedience to the Lord God, who had given them everything freely.

The suave stranger inquired further, "But why? What's the reason you can't eat that most delicious fruit?" Eve probably rolled her eyes looking at the sky searching for the right words. Finally she said, "All I know is, that we will surely die if we eat it or touch it." The stranger probably chuckled and laughed deep and low. Eve must have been both repelled and attracted to him to continue this dialogue.

The stranger assured Eve, "You won't surely die." He suggested that God simply desired to keep them in subjection. For the first time, Eve felt a sense of limitation. She probably thought it would be a grand thing to be as wise as God. The stranger's reasoning was vividly enticing!

"Eve, are you afraid?" whispered Satan softly. Eve slowly crept closer to the forbidden tree. It was beautiful to look at. The fruit seemed irresistible. She lifted her hand and let her fingers curl around the cool skin of that sumptuous fruit. One gentle tug and the twig sprang upward with a solitary broken stem. The prize felt good in her warm palm. In one ungovernable moment, Eve raised the fruit to her mouth and tasted its heavenly nectar. Pride refused to let her turn back now. A fateful decisive moment had lingered gingerly and then the sweetness turned bitter. And the bitter taste remained.

When Adam returned from his walk, he noticed Eve standing by the forbidden tree with a half-eaten fruit in her hand. His countenance must have caused her to blush for the first time. With one glance, Adam understood what his wife had done. The garden was eerily quiet and the two of them stood alone. Together they looked at the fruit in Eve's hand, then they looked at each other.

Adam probably wondered out loud, "Why, Eve?" and Eve probably asked, "Why not you too, Adam?"

She told Adam about the stranger and how the fruit was so enticing and how she dared to do a thing Adam never thought of doing! She had tasted the wisdom of heaven while he ate earthly food. The intimate relationship between them was not so close anymore. Adam felt isolated; it was as if a bottomless abyss opened up between them, an unbridgeable chasm. The pain in his eyes was desperate. What could he possibly do? Against his will, he wondered how the fruit tasted.

Adam then slowly took the fruit from Eve's hand and tasted it. A sudden sadness overwhelmed the lonely husband and his wife. Surrounding them was a feeling of something accusing, punishing, and inescapable. Feeling as never before, they wrestled with their new situation until God called from the twilight, "Adam! Where are you, Adam?" Suddenly, they did not feel the presence of God anymore; what they felt was the presence of evil.

Another new emotion washed over them; they were afraid. Adam managed to reply in a quivering voice, "I heard your voice, and I was afraid because I was naked, so I hid." The silence that followed was deafening. A sorrowful moment lingered, then God gently asked, "Adam, who told you that you were naked?", but Adam had no answer.

But then, with treason in his voice, Adam blamed God for giving him a wife, and the wife for giving him the fruit. With one indictment, he cast upon someone else, even his nearest and dearest, the responsibility for his own wrong use of his free will. Eve soon discovered the bitter truth behind the serpent's lie, "You won't surely die."

God provided them a coat of animal skins to cover themselves. It was a gift of grace – through sacrifice, a sacrifice of blood. Adam and Eve were ushered out of the Garden of Eden into a cursed world. God was needed now more than ever. They were given a reprieve, not a pardon.

Adam and Eve had only to tend the garden and be obedient. They couldn't do it for the same reason you can't do it now. Sin is quick, deceptive, painful, and deadly. Sin won the battle, but it's God who wins the war. The effects of sin are not always immediate. Adam and Eve faced ignominious expulsion and learned quickly that God meant what He said. There is no substitute for communion with God, as inward peace becomes a reality and fear is banished. God is immutable; He hasn't changed His position. Sin is offensive to Him and always will be.

God will remove our sin when we let Him. His plan is for us to experience freedom from sin by trusting Him in obedience. The long-promised Messiah can show us the way of forgiveness in a world drenched in sin. God is preparing a sin-free kingdom for us in Heaven.

The account of Lot living in Sodom is another illustration of sin in the old world. Sodom was a city filled with depravity, and depravity offends God. The city's stench had filled God's nostrils. God had set about to destroy the city of Sodom and others with it.

Lot's father died when he was young, leaving his uncle Abraham to serve as a role model. Both were wealthy and decided to settle down after traveling from Ur of the Chaldees. Abraham settled in the land of Canaan. Lot chose to settle in the plains of Jordan, and pitched his tent toward Sodom. Being influenced by Abraham, Lot didn't particularly like Sodom's reputation, but he was very partial to making money trading in sheep and cattle with its inhabitants.

Before long, Lot had blended into the culture of Sodom and completely lost the sense of purpose Abraham had. Caught up with making money, Lot failed to see the consequences of his actions. Lot became blind to what his selfish behavior was doing to his family or his relationship with Abraham. God was slowly being pushed out of Lot's life.

Even God's patience has a limit. God sent two angels to Sodom to remove Lot and his family, and then deliver judgment. Lot hesitated when the angels told him it was time to leave. He would lose everything he had built over the years - houses, flocks, herds - all would be gone. While family pulled in opposite directions, Lot wavered. Lost between longing for his possessions and God's grace, his faith and his doubt fought each other while God waited. But God couldn't wait for long; the decision was cast, and time had run out for the city of Sodom. Mercy had been extended and mercy had been refused.

Finally, the angels led Lot, his wife, and his two daughters to safety outside the city. That day God destroyed the cities of Sodom and Gomorrah and others with fire and brimstone. Warned not to look back at the destruction, Lot's wife turned back to see her former life one final time and disobedience caused her death. She was immortalized as a pillar of salt!

God refuses to let you go without giving you every chance to respond to the grace He extends. Many feel that Lot did not deserve God's mercy. He was selfish, materialistic, and procrastinating. Maybe Lot was morally superior; but because he fraternized with the ungodly, when he finally took a stand his credibility was of no value. When sin becomes your lifestyle, you are no longer an effective witness for God.

It is important where you live, work, and play because the orbit of evil is a dangerous place. Perhaps Lot lived too close to Sodom to resist it. We can live too close to temptation with similar consequences. God showed extreme patience in letting all who wanted to escape avoid the coming destruction. God openly showed His anger at the sin that was so flagrant, and at the people who refused His mercy.

Learn a lesson from Lot. Don't let your environment shape you; be proactive and shape the environment around you. Jesus did it; you can, too. Once Lot knew of the danger, he was in peril if he remained in the city. Don't leave your heart in sin, and then look back after you've been rescued. Don't delay when God is calling you: there may be no time for second chances.

"So when God destroyed the cities of the plain,
he remembered Abraham,
and he brought Lot out of the catastrophe."
Genesis 19:29

Abraham prayed for Lot, and God remembered Abraham's petitions. What if Abraham had not prayed for Lot? What would have been his fate? Would God have spared him? Who is praying for you? For whom are you praying? Whom might God save because of your prayers? God said the prayers of a righteous man are powerful and effective. (see James 5:16) We are not to give up. Prayer changes lives and it can change God's heart.

Sin is relentless. It travels across time and cultures like a plague. No one is immune to its assault. Christ was tempted after a long period of fasting. Satan attacked Christ in His weakened state, when he was most apt to sin. At each temptation, Christ quoted Scripture in response to the devil. The tempter was real, and the temptation was real. Christ was human, capable of sin and vulnerable, but he resisted and sinned not.

Christ had never felt the weight of sin before He became one of us. Even though He remained sinless, He wanted to know you, your pain, your misery, your struggles, and your emotions. He wanted to be a part of you so you could become part of Him. He came for you, He served you, He died for you, and at His second coming, He will come back for you.

Jesus relinquished a heavenly crown for a crown of thorns. He did this for you, so you could eat at His table. He chose pain and suffering so you could see Him in glory. He endured the ugly sin of the world for you – a sinner – so you wouldn't be separated from God. It was the only way to forgive you of all your transgressions.

The life of Christ was not meant to entertain and amuse, it was meant to illuminate, teach, and inspire. It was meant to be a sacrifice for you. Jesus endured temptation to show us that Satan can be overcome with Scripture, and show that He was capable of being tempted just as we are.

In Matthew 27:46, while Jesus was on the cross, He cried out, "My God, My God, why have you forsaken me?" Christ invoked every word of Psalm 22 as he fought for breath while sweating blood out of his torn flesh. Jesus had to endure the heat and flies, the insults from the crowd, and the intense pain his heart was experiencing. Imagine, God's son in human flesh, speaking God's Word to a lost and dying world while pinned to a Roman cross! This was indeed the ultimate sacrifice for atonement. An innocent man dying for the very ones who killed him!

What do you see when you see a cross? Do you only see the intersection of vertical and horizontal lines? Do you see a metaphor of earth reaching up to heaven? Do you see a torture device created by a carpenter? Do you want to turn away because it represents an emblem of pain and suffering? Iron spikes driven through tanned calloused hands! Why? Why would God let humans do this to His son? Was there any other way? No!

God's divine plan allowed sin to enter the world. Knowing sin would attach itself to us, God made provisions for our restoration. Before the foundation of the world was laid, a Savior was planned. One who would clean the stain caused by sin. You are vitally important to God. You are also important to the devil. Both want you for entirely different reasons.

Satan wants you to live his kind of life, not God's. Satan wants you to think sin is pleasant and good, even desirable. You are of great interest to him. He wants you to follow him willingly, but if not, he will use any deception necessary to snare you. In Luke chapter 22, Jesus tells Simon Peter of Satan's intentions, "Simon, Simon, Satan has asked to sift you like wheat!" Recall Satan asking God to test His servant Job? Satan had the same desire to test Simon, the disciples, and others. Even you are on his list.

In today's world there are so many temptations, and with the field broadening daily, what are we to do? To escape the temptation and the sin you may fall into, turn to Jesus. Of course you've heard this a million times. You would not keep hearing it if it were not essential for your survival! God desperately wants you to hear this message: <u>Stop Sinning!</u>

Sin is a whirlpool that pulls you deeper into itself so that you can't see beyond its currents. Focus on what God has given you, not on what you don't have. You have God's Word to guide you through any hardship, any temptation, any doubt. Scripture gives you truth, hope, joy, peace, and all of God's promises. The world offers you attractive temptations that challenge your discretion and obedience. The tempter offers you nothing of substance, nothing lasting, nothing lifesaving. There is logic here. Be self-controlled and alert.

Simon Peter remembered what Jesus said to him about Satan's intentions. Thirty years later, in the last years of his life, Peter wrote a letter encouraging those facing temptation and persecution. He told them, "Your enemy the devil prowls around like a roaring lion looking for someone to devour. Resist him, standing firm in the faith, because you know that your brothers and sisters throughout the world are undergoing the same kind of sufferings" (1 Peter 5:8-9).

Temptation is real and it will visit you. Ready yourself. Don't be discouraged; the testing of your faith develops patience. There are two things you can count on: your faith will be tested, and your faithfulness will be rewarded. These two are tied together like a Gordian knot.

The pain in your life is the result of sin. Memorize this fact! It is worth repeating: the pain in your life is the result of sin. The presence of sin is everywhere, but it is possible to limit its impact. Know your areas of weakness, build some defenses before temptation calls, know and utilize Scripture. A friend or accountability partner to pray with can prop you up in times of weakness. Jesus prayed frequently; should we do any less? Remember, even Satan knows Scripture. But he chooses not to obey it.

You are called to be strong and mature. Your life has purpose, and your choices matter to those who love you. God loves you. You are more than food for a stalking lion; you are created in His image and called to do good works.

Jesus was crucified on an old rugged cross. Right until the end, Jesus claimed to be the Messiah. Any mortal would have conjured up a story to get off that brutal cross and save himself. Jesus came to fulfill prophecy. Jesus came freely to save us. Seek Him; He will reveal Himself to you. He is in the space between you and these pages. He's asked you to come to Heaven. It's not all about sin and pain and death. From God's perspective, it's all about you!

Chapter Six

Decisive Convergence

Who are you in the context of God's love? You are His beloved. You are His pride and joy. You are His creation, made to be near and dear to Him. Let truth's meaning, heaven's purity, and the garden's peace fill your existence. Let God's spirit teach you and angels restore you. Let God deliver wisdom, leading, guidance, and direction. Become a profile in courage, step out on faith, and let Christ be the example you strive for.

You have a place in God's plan and He wants to use you. Your talents might be obvious - a gifted singer, actor, writer, athlete, or scientist. Maybe your creative gifts are not so obvious. Perhaps you're an organizer, a volunteer, cook, sailor, soldier, salesman, or parent. We need all these people. As a matter of fact, we couldn't survive and evolve without them. The Bible clearly states that we are all equally important; no one is more important than another. Our unique gifts are not meant to separate us from each other - they are meant to bring us together. We are teachers, servers, encouragers, and listeners. We are called to both lead and follow, according to God's will for us.

With our garden identity a distant memory, what manner of behavior should we strive for now? Our original relationship was with God the Father. That relationship was broken when sin separated the created from the creator. Our current relationship with God the Father is one of wrath as a result of sin. This relationship can only be restored through a mediator bringing both sides together again. We can have peace with God the Father, but only through Jesus Christ – our mediator.

Through our constant searching, God guides and directs. He never forces our decisions but instead gives us reasons to choose the greater good; to choose as Joshua in the Old Testament chose – to serve the God of Abraham, Isaac, and Jacob.

This is where we want to be; confident decision makers led by God. But how do we get there? We must recognize that God uses imperfect people. We need to allow the Holy Spirit to transform us and draw us to a right relationship with God. He is the potter; we are merely the lifeless clay.

God has given you free will to choose both the content and direction of your life, but there is a caveat you should be aware of: free will carries with it awesome responsibilities and unimagined challenges. You have free will to make multiple choices, including choosing whom you will serve. But exercise caution, for a single choice could prove to be the sum of all your decisions. Be fore-warned, choosing your god or the true God is not a decision made lightly through ignorance or indifference. This is a decision that carries enormous weight. Our decisions need precedent, a history, an example to follow.

People are often afraid to make an important decision. In life, you either make a decision or a decision will be made for you. Indecision is not an option. *Not* to make a decision *is* to make a decision! Our parents and teachers spend a great deal of time and attention teaching us as children how to make rational, thoughtful, and intelligent choices. As some get older they jettison all this valu-able instruction and become the blind led by the blind. The Bible teaches us through a common sense approach, "If a blind man leads a blind man, both will fall into a pit" (Matthew 15:14).

We have people who are self-indulgent and self-centered telling us how to conduct business, what to believe, and even who to vote for. Should we take their advice because we like them, or should we be objective and impartial, and scrutinize the facts and circum-stances ourselves? Maybe following the herd isn't always in our best interests. God did say; let *us* reason *together*. (see Isaiah 1:18)

Some people will always have their own best interest at heart and then want you to support their decisions.

By living according to how they feel and what they want, these people's desires crash headlong into reality. They chase after pleasure, danger, fame, and fortune. The major issues of life become leisure, possessions, and anything self-serving. Feelings and emotions drive their daily decisions. Regardless of all the options available, they gravitate to darkness. The Bible instructs us to quit being selfish. We are to desire superior choices. The Bible is our ultimate standard, not what's right in our own eyes.

In life we all have to make choices. In doing so, we will inevitably make some mistakes. At times you will be forced to make decisions before knowing all the facts, or the alternatives, or the consequences. Admitting that mistakes are a fact of life, how do we summon the courage and wisdom to make tough decisions? Fate is not what drives men to their decisions and actions, but rather the human condition. William Shakespeare put it succinctly in his play, *Julius Caesar*, when he wrote:

> "The fault, dear Brutus, lies not in our stars,
> but in ourselves!"

There will come times in your life when certain situations and circumstances will test what you're made of. Events will converge on your mediocre life that will thrust you into heavenly realms. You will feel the presence of God and the devil simultaneously. Your inner self will ignite with a compulsion for action – to run, to shout, to do something. A decisive moment is about to take place. You will be caught up in its vortex, unable to delay. Your adrenaline will flow, your heart will beat faster, your breathing will quicken, and your central cortex will be an electrical firestorm. The stage is being set for action.

A decisive moment is when a decision must be made on the spot – instantly. It can be compared to being scared suddenly. Psychologists have determined that when we're frightened we have an instant reaction. By reflex we choose either a fight or flight response. It can be viscerally intense and paralyzing. Indecision is Satan's open door. Indecision is fatal!

When a confluence of opposing ideas battle for our attention, how do we decide rightly, conclusively, and firmly what is in our best interest and in the center of God's will? How do we seek help to make the wise choice? How do we prepare for the really tough decisions? They will come. Have you decided to be prepared?

There will come a time when you're faced with a decisive convergence. A moment when you bring everything you've learned and everything you've been taught into a single defining moment. You will put right and wrong into perspective, your feelings and emotions will reason instantly with your intellect. You will make a decision based on everything your life experiences have taught you. The defining moment will occur when you take a stand, when an event occurs that forces you to make a commitment and define your beliefs.

Your crucible might be a death in the family, a financial disaster, a divorce, or when your health fails. Some will question God and put Him on trial, and some will seek God's consolation and ask for understanding. Everyone will face defining moments in life. These decisive moments will strengthen their faith or put distance between themselves and God.

In the Old Testament, the prophet Daniel faced a decisive convergence that set an example we should follow today. Taken captive by the Babylonians, he was forced to leave his hometown of Jerusalem and settle in Babylon, five hundred miles away. Once there, he had to learn a new language and new customs, eat strange foods, and trust in God implicitly: a hard thing for anyone, but especially for Daniel, who was only a teenager. Decisions had to be made quickly, not only for survival, but for the far-reaching consequences. Prepared for the tough decisions from his youth, Daniel struggled to remain in God's will. What a profile in courage this young man displayed!

The King of Babylon was preparing Daniel and others for service in his court of advisors. One test required that Daniel and his friends follow the king's orders expressly. Early on it was decided that Daniel was to eat the king's meat and drink the king's wine. This particular request was challenged by Daniel; possibly due to the conditions set. First – it was probably an unclean or forbidden food according to Jewish law. Second – it was likely not prepared according to Jewish law. Third – it might have been meat that had been sacrificed to pagan idols.

> "But Daniel purposed in his heart
> that he would not defile himself
> with the portion of the king's meat,
> nor with the wine which he drank."
> Daniel 1:8 KJV

Even though Daniel was absorbed into a land that did not follow God's laws, Daniel was faithful to obey them himself. Daniel and his friends had already made up their minds to follow the laws given to Moses rather than *become* Babylonian. Daniel's decision was made prior to the challenge. Like Abraham, he decided to be faithful first, then face any obstacles life might bring.

Who taught Daniel to be obedient to Jewish law? Why was he steadfast in obeying it? He could have quietly acquiesced and nobody would have questioned his service to the king. His motives were entrenched and fixed. Children follow the examples set by their parents (see Genesis 26:7; 12:10-14; 20:1-4; Proverbs 1:8). Daniel decided in advance what he was going to do. He found the means to obey God and influence others, without being influenced or persuaded by the culture.

Business schools teach how to minimize investment and maximize profits. Law schools instruct how to argue a defense and follow the letter of the law. Medical schools train interns to prepare for life and death decisions. In the military, young recruits are trained to fight in battle conditions. They drill and exercise and compete with one another to hone their skills. Along with building a military-oriented mind, they forge deeply ingrained habits. Learning how to fight before the battle helps prevent injury and ultimately, defeat. It's too late to learn those skills and habits in the heat of battle. Preparation is everything. If you're ambushed, there was probably fault in the planning.

Deep down we all know why we have fire drills in school. Why there are lifeboats and life jackets on ships. Why there are warning labels on bottles of medicine. These steps have been taken because tragedy has occurred and innocent life was needlessly lost. Making the necessary decisions before an emergency reduces heartbreak and suffering.

Others might not follow our example, but they will see and remember it. Whether an Old Testament Jew or a New Testament Christian, we are obligated to be distinctive and find a way to make following God attractive. If our faith can't be tested now and then, can it be trusted? Your decisions affect others. Make a habit of deciding wisely. Don't try to reason with the serpent like Eve did. Don't be so easily beguiled. You have a Creator who desires to help, love, and protect you; be receptive, don't let your pride push Him aside. Seek God's advice; start looking at *how* your decisions affect others. Paul's first letter to the Corinthian church is a travel guide to becoming a responsible decision maker.

Paul emphasizes that whatever we do, "...do it all for the glory of God" (1 Corinthians 10:31). If we are to be Christlike, then our conduct should conform to the characteristics *and* behaviors of Christ. In making decisions, we should give serious consideration to the effect those decisions will have on our witness for God. Will it be beneficial or destructive to our example as a believer in Christ? Will the decision diminish my own faith or interfere in any way with the faith of another? We must resolve to carefully weigh our decision-making process to ensure that we do nothing that enriches us at the expense of others or that hinders spiritual growth. If there is any doubt, err on the side of righteousness.

It is easier to resist temptation if your convictions are fixed before temptation presents itself. We get into unimaginable trouble because we haven't determined beforehand where to draw the line. Before a crippling decisive moment happens, make your commitments early in life, so when the serpent appears, you will be prepared. Recognize the temptation before it takes control. Deciding to become a Christian is not without consequences or responsibilities, but not to become a Christian is merely delayed suicide.

God has endowed us with the ability to reason. We can be influenced by television, books, movies, and peers, but choosing the still small voice of God is up to us. The gifts God has given us are sleeping quietly within us. We need to awaken them and take possession of these gifts. Christ shared our human experience completely. He used the same gifts available to us.

Christ moved from being taught to teaching others. He transitioned from the basics to developing a depth of understanding. He chose spiritual challenges rather than entertainment. He moved from opinions and hearsay to study and confidence. He went from feelings and emotions to confidence, maturity, and an active faith. It's not just good feelings and positive thinking; it is knowing that God is in control, our destiny is sure, and victory over sin and death is certain. Satan has tremendous influence, but God is sovereign.

All the gifts living in you were given to you by your creator. He calls you to give Him glory by cultivating these gifts to their highest capacity. God's gifts differ in nature, power, and effectiveness according to His wishes; not according to your faith. By ignoring your gifts, you ignore a gesture of God's love.

Christ invested the gifts God gave Him. It's time to move out of your comfortable position and train yourself to run the race of life. Training takes practice, energy, dedication, and vision. Living the Christian life requires all your energy. This spiritual exercise will allow you to grow in faith and character. The dividends are a place of eternal rest and a crown. It is citizenship in Christ's kingdom and eternal presence with our creator; all this through the simple act of obedience. So be watchful, keep your eyes on the prize.

Your salvation is important to God. He took humanness upon Himself so you could understand Him. He is anxious to share in your gifts and decisions. Whether you are a missionary, a teacher, or an encourager, your life touches countless others. You are called to be Christ's ambassador. It is your privilege and your responsibility to participate in life. So don't wander through life at random, be Spirit-filled and walk purposefully in God's will.

You have worth. You have talents. You have free will and critical decision- making ability. You are integral to the work of God's kingdom. Share with others what God has given you. If you have experienced pain, comfort those who are suffering. If you have abundance, give a portion to those less fortunate. If you understand the plan of salvation, give to others the greatest gift the world has ever experienced.

God has shared everything with us - His only begotten son, His Holy Spirit, His creation, and His abundance. What have we shared with God? What have we shared with others? God has generously made us stewards of His largesse and given us everything needed to make this a purpose-filled life. Having everything, we should make the decision to share God – with others. Don't be selfish; it's not all about you.

Chapter 7

Under the Influence

W e know that powerful forces are at work in this world. Some
are encouraging us to do good, some tempting us to do evil.
The genesis of sin is still with us and seeks to control us. There is
no doubt our lives are influenced on a corporate level by angels.
But what influences our lives on an individual basis? Some public
opinion polls say that, on the whole, people are basically good down
deep inside. Is this true? Is this false? Is there a DNA marker in our
gene pool that imprints us as mostly good or mostly bad? Is there
within us a moral compass that allows us to act good, all on our
own?

Mankind has argued this type of sophistry for centuries. We
tend to measure ourselves by ourselves. The Bible tells us that this
method of self-examination is not only faulty but dangerous. The
Bible has something to say about our goodness. In Luke 18:19, Jesus
said, "no one is good – except God alone." Isaiah 64:6 tells us that
we are all unclean, "and all our righteousness is as filthy rags." We
cannot approach God based on our goodness because we have none.
How then can we possibly gain an audience with God to even plead
for mercy? God has made provisions. God can be approached if we
come in the name of His son.

In the eyes of each other we may appear suspicious, but other-
wise acceptable. In the eyes of God, our present condition is like an
outlaw, a trespasser, a beggar. While we're definitely noticed, direct

access is very restricted. Our position is unchanged; we're outside of redemption seeking entry. Our condition is helpless and deteriorating. Romans 3:23 says, "For all have sinned and come short of the glory of God." Romans 6:23 takes our condition and adds a measure of judgment by saying, "for the wages of sin is death." It's at this point we recognize our situation is not only dire but life threatening. How can we possibly escape the inevitable?

In the Old Testament, those who had sinned could take a bird or animal that was ceremonially clean to the high priest at the temple, and have the animal offered up on the altar as a sacrifice to atone, or make up for, the sin. This system worked insomuch as it covered the sin and the person was given a reprieve. In truth, the sacrifice only covered the sin; it never fully took the sin away and made the individual sinless. The root problem lies in the fact that Adam directly transferred sin to each member of the human race. Romans 5:12 says, "Therefore just as sin entered the world through one man, and death through sin, and in this way death came to all men, because all have sinned." Are we responsible for Adam's sin committed thousands of years ago? Yes - because the sin nature is still with us, we still sin.

In the New Testament, the Bible describes a man named John, the son of Elizabeth and Zechariah. He was a cousin of Jesus and had a ministry in the desert of Judea. People came from all over to hear this *voice crying in the wilderness.* John dressed in camel skins and ate wild locusts and honey. His manner was reminiscent of Elijah the prophet. John preached that the people should repent and be baptized with water. He earned the nickname of *John the Baptist.* When Jesus came to the Jordan River where John was baptizing, something extraordinary happened. When John saw Jesus approaching, he paused and made an announcement to everyone there, "Look, the Lamb of God, who takes away the sin of the world!" (John 1:29).

John was speaking a magnificent truth on many levels. When John spoke of *the Lamb,* he was referring to history (the Passover lamb, Exodus 12:3), and to prophecy (the Messiah, Isaiah 53:7). History and prophecy are linked together in this metaphor. John mentions the sin of the world, not just the sins of Israel (see Isaiah 53:4-12; I John 2:2). For the first time since the Garden of Eden, the human race had a chance to be restored to innocence without the guilt and stain of sin. An influence had appeared on the world scene that would forever change the way we live.

The New Testament gospels record a brief outline of the life and works of Jesus. The four gospel writers (Matthew, Mark, Luke, and John) record their personal time spent with Christ. They provide a glance at the most controversial person ever to touch our lives. These eyewitness accounts were written from twenty-five to fifty years *after* the crucifixion of Jesus in Jerusalem. The testimonies are from their own experiences and in their own words. What influenced them and changed their lives can and will influence you. To what degree depends entirely upon you.

Matthew wrote from the Jewish viewpoint. He records the royal genealogy of Christ in the first seventeen verses, presenting Christ as King. A king by birth, not by the will of the people. Matthew writes repeatedly... *"That it might be fulfilled as was spoken by the prophet"*. The Jewish mind understood the importance of fulfilled prophecy, and that the anointed one must be a teacher well versed in the Old Testament and familiar with the customs of the Jews. Matthew, being a Jew himself, adroitly but exquisitely presented the case for Christ as the Messiah to a Jewish audience.

Mark's discourse was directed to the Romans. The Romans knew and cared nothing about the Old Testament Scriptures and its prophecies concerning a messiah. Mark presented Christ as a remarkable leader, a powerful man with authority, and as someone who possessed extraordinary powers. Mark offered Jesus as an authority figure who was filled with deeds and actions, not just words alone. The Romans weren't concerned about a prophet or a king, but a man who could meet every human need - that was a person of great interest. Every Roman could appreciate a leader of men who not only spoke with authority, but could empathize and show compassion. This frightened the Roman authorities because Jesus was not under their control.

Luke was a Greek doctor writing to his fellow countrymen who were lovers of beauty, culture, and lofty ideas. Appealing to the student and the seeker, Luke detailed the birth of Jesus, His childhood, His ministry of healing and comforting the sick and ailing.

Being a physician, Luke was very precise in the details and accuracy of his writings. He wrote to those desiring truth and happiness, a Gentile presenting a savior to those outside of Judaism.

John was directing his letter to everyone: Jew, Gentile, freeman, slave, man or woman. He wanted every person reading his account to know that Jesus is the Christ, the Son of God. His gospel is filled with accounts of Jesus' divine character and the marvelous miracles accomplished. John gave us the passage that *whosoever* believes on the Lord Jesus has eternal life. His reasoned approach was to the masses, "In the beginning was the Word, and the Word was with God, and the Word was God" (John 1:1). Salvation was directed to the Jews, but after rejecting Christ, salvation was now available to *whosoever*.

When these men met Jesus of Nazareth, their lives were influenced forever. They helped set the kingdom of heaven in motion. Jesus told them that they would become *fishers of men*. He instructed them to spread out like ripples on a pond, telling everyone about His works and His witness; first from Jerusalem, then to the area of Judea, then to the whole world. From His birth through His ministry to His gruesome death and glorious resurrection - it was without question the greatest story ever recorded.

Jesus performed some of the most spectacular miracles the world had ever witnessed. The blind were given their sight, the lame were able to walk, the deaf were able to hear, lepers were cured, and the dead were raised! These were no mere claims, but recorded eyewitness accounts of signs and wonders. These miracles were Jesus' credentials to the unbelieving. Jesus told the Jews who wanted to kill him, "even though you do not believe me, believe the miracles, that you may know and understand that the Father is in me, and I in the Father" (John 10:38). This infuriated the Jewish leaders of that day. Like people today, they could ignore His words, but they could not deny the miracles being performed. You can ignore the Bible and stick your head in the sand like an ostrich, but its influence will eventually touch you or someone you love. Because the Bible is alive, it will draw people to Christ.

Eyewitnesses record in detail the agonizing death of Jesus, His burial, *and* His resurrection from the grave. Those who came to Jerusalem for the Passover could view the crucifixion; the Roman soldiers witnessed what happened; most of the angels watched and waited; and God the Father watched as the Passover Lamb opened the doors of heaven.

Jesus' body would be taken down from the cross and laid in a borrowed tomb. But it would not stay there long because Jesus' body would not see decay (see Psalms 16:10; Acts 13:34-37), there would be no ashes to ashes, no dust to dust. The incarnate and immortal would remain that way.

His resurrection would be so life changing, hardly anything would be the same again. His death changed the way we keep time today. Two thousand years later life is recorded as B.C., before Christ; and A.D., *anno Domini*, Latin for in the year of our Lord. Never in the history of the world had anyone come back from the grave – on his own! For an earthshaking moment, time stood still. Daniel's prophetic clock stopped ticking after sixty-nine weeks and won't start ticking again until the Second Coming. A portal of grace had opened and called to everyone, "behold the Lamb."

Great religions have had their leaders - Buddha, Confucius, Mohammed, and Joseph Smith - but even to this day these men remain...in their tombs. Which one foretold his death and how it would happen? Who gave up his life willingly as a sacrifice for many? Who triumphed over death and now holds the keys of death and Hades? Who said he would come back from the grave? Who promised he would come again in glory? Who is alive and sitting at the right hand of God? Who is the one true God? Go ahead, whisper His name, God is listening. Now, who lives in you?

The Old Testament prophets predicted the coming of the messiah, and all of Israel waited eagerly. The religious leaders of Jesus' day read the scriptures and understood them, but when He came to fulfill those very same prophesies, they had their eyes and ears closed and missed Him!

They missed Him plain and simple. They missed the prophet Micah's prediction that the messiah would be born in Bethlehem (see Micah 5:2). They missed that He would be the seed of Abraham (see Genesis 12:3; 18:18), of the tribe of Judah (see Genesis 49:10), of the seed of Jacob (see Numbers 24:17-19), of the seed of David (see Jeremiah 23:5; Isaiah 11:10), and a prophet like Moses (see

Deuteronomy 18:15-19). They missed the fact that Galilee would be the first area of the messiah's ministry (see Isaiah 9:1-8). They missed the fact that the messiah would perform miracles (see Isaiah 35:5-6).

Even though a man born blind was given his sight by Jesus, the religious rulers wanted to condemn Jesus for performing a miracle on the Sabbath! They discarded the miracle entirely and charged Jesus with *breaking the Sabbath*. They wanted to stone Jesus to death for being a Sabbath-breaker! The blind man could see the hypocrisy and the injustice, why couldn't the sighted?

The religious leaders heard about everything that Jesus was doing. Every word and deed was done in public view; where He traveled, with whom He ate, and who His disciples were. Still, the leaders missed all the signals; the messiah entering the temple with authority (see Malachi 3:1), entering Jerusalem on a donkey (see Zechariah 9:9), even the portrait that the messiah would be pierced (see Zechariah 12:10). Pierced by the very Romans who would find no fault in Him!

Saul was a religious leader of high rank, a zealous Pharisee, who brutally persecuted the followers of Jesus. One day on the road to Damascus, Saul was struck by a blinding light, and heard a voice from heaven speaking directly to him. It was the voice of Jesus asking, "Why are you persecuting me?" Saul had no answer. Blinded and helpless for three days, he deftly contemplated his circumstances until realizing the voice from heaven was right. Like Job's friends, Saul had been sincere, but sincerely wrong.

God changed Saul's name to Paul, and from then on, the Lord would use Paul to bring the message of salvation to the Gentiles and their kings. A Jew among the elite, Paul would herald the prophecies that Jesus fulfilled, the miracles witnessed by many, and recall the eyewitnesses of the resurrection. A devout and learned Jew, Paul himself also missed the coming of the messiah. Writing one third of the New Testament, his passionate discourses would help unlock the mysteries of who Jesus really was.

Jesus began His earthly ministry when he set out from Nazareth, his childhood home. Baptized by John the Baptist in the Jordan River, and tempted by Satan in the wilderness, Jesus traveled and ministered in Judea and Samaria, then returned to Galilee. Jesus' ministry was summed up in Luke 19:10, by these simple words, one syllable each:

> "For the Son of Man came to seek and save
> what was lost."

It became apparent early in Jesus' ministry that many did not want to be sought out or found. When Jesus returned to Nazareth, his hometown, the local residents could not bring themselves to believe in His message. Jesus came to them as a prophet, but they couldn't see past the man they knew; the oldest son of Mary and Joseph. Jesus did very few miracles in his hometown because of the people's unbelief. Jeremiah, the Old Testament prophet, experienced the same type of rejection (see Jeremiah 12:5-6). If you can't see God in your life, could it be because of unbelief? Is seeing believing? The two blind men to whom Jesus gave sight in Matthew 20 didn't have that luxury.

About the second year into His public ministry, Jesus spoke near Capernaum, on a hillside, and gave us the famous Sermon on the Mount found in Matthew, chapters 5 through 7. It was the greatest discourse in history. Jesus stated his position on various topics. He spoke of the Old Testament law, anger, divorce, revenge, enemies, the poor, money, worry, and most important, the way to heaven - all the affairs critical to everyday life. The crowds were enormous and expectations were high. Jesus did not disappoint. He never disappointed.

Sounding like an Old Testament prophet, His message was simple, direct, and authoritative. Have faith in God, remember God's promises and mercies, be obedient, and seek the kingdom of heaven first. Then Jesus turned their comfortable world on end, and challenged them - don't hate your enemies, love them! Don't love money, for loving it is the root of all kinds of evil. Avoid anger and hatred; don't lust after others, be faithful; show mercy and love to others. Pay your taxes, give to the poor without expecting accolades; don't worry about everything – trust God. Quit complaining, quit criticizing others, quit being selfish, love God, and love your neighbor as yourself.

Nobody ever said things like this before. His words stirred something deep within His listeners. They couldn't get enough of Jesus' teachings. These were words to live your life by. There was a way to be happy and content with life, even under a repressive Roman rule. Jesus was teaching the multitudes that there could be joy in life. There is a way to live life every day without misery and oppression. He wanted to drive home the point: stop focusing on yourselves, remember how much God loves you and wants to draw near to you. This life is temporary; start thinking about the afterlife. You need to be ready for it, prepare for it, expect it, look for it, welcome it, and embrace it. You need to yearn for it.

Ecclesiastes 3:1-2 says "There is a time for everything, and a season for every activity under heaven: a time to be born and a time to die." Barely three years had passed and Christ's ministry was almost at an end. Jesus had come at a specific time and for a specific purpose. Now with His work almost done, His brief life was about to culminate in prophetic destiny. Intelligent design was at work. The confluence of events that was about to unfold was no accident. The Law of Moses was about to be transformed into the Grace of God. The influence of Jesus would cast a shadow of hope across the whole world – in the form of a cross.

The prophecies of Jesus' birth were predicted centuries in advance and not one of the predictions failed to come true. The ancient prophecies said He would be meek and mild (see Isaiah 42:2-3), and that He would minister to the Gentiles (see Isaiah 49:1-8). They predicted He would be forsaken by His disciples (see Zechariah 13:7), smitten (see Isaiah 50:6), and that He would be pierced (see Zechariah 12:10). All were fulfilled to the very letter.

His life was a tapestry of immense complexity. His birth was announced by angels; he was born in a manger, visited by Magi, raised by poor parents in a little crossroads town tucked into the backwoods of Galilee; could His life have been anything but destiny? The little town of Nazareth would forever wonder who He really was. His life and words influence us to this day. Born innocent, and having died without sin, He lived a good life to show that it could be done. All He really wanted to do was to seek and save the lost. *Seek and save you!*

Has Jesus had an influence on you, your life, your work, and your play? Have you prevented Him *from*, or permitted Him *to*? It is your decision. Before it is too late, remember that it's still all about you.

Chapter 8

Narrow's the Road

When do you plan to die? The exact day isn't necessary; just the month and year will be fine. What, you don't know? Have you given it much thought? You do realize that the *when* is not as important as the *how*! After all, we live so close to the future, it is foolish not to plan for it. Newspapers print obituaries daily, hospitals and nursing homes give comfort to those near death, and cemeteries are always expanding to accommodate more. It is time to give it more than a fleeting thought. Death is a giant whirlpool drawing everyone into its grasp. Depending on where you are in the tunnel vortex, you may be gently moving or spinning at the speed of light. Either way we are all being pulled toward our destiny.

The Bible says in Psalms that the average length of our days is threescore and ten years. A brief seventy years. Maybe. Ask anyone past the age of sixty or seventy and they will tell you the brutal but unexpected truth; life goes by so very quickly! When you look at history in retrospect, a hundred years here, a thousand years there, the Romans were correct in their assessment: *tempus fugit*. (Time flees!). Your life is akin to a giant carpet being rolled up slowly. Like it is being prepared to be moved to a new location; either for cleaning and restoration to be proudly displayed, or worse - discarded. James, the half-brother of Jesus, said in his epistle, "What is your life? You are a mist that appears for a little while and then vanishes" (James 4:14).

If we are only here for a little while, then shouldn't we make a serious attempt at finding out what life is all about? Shouldn't we live every day as though it could be our last? Shouldn't we earnestly seek God and discover exactly what is expected from us? Life is a gift from the creator, and any day we could be called upon to return this gift and give an accounting. Be assured that mortality is guaranteed.

The statistics are unfailingly grim: one out of every one person - dies! It may sound unnatural, but death is a completely natural occurrence. After sin was ushered into the world at the Garden of Eden, the natural order of things changed. Death spread to all things - the fish of the sea, the animal kingdom, birds of the air, and all human life. Everything will surely die. Satan had baited a trap in the garden and caught a whole world brimming with life! The critical question we should address is not when death will come, but rather what happens to us after death.

People have contemplated the afterlife throughout history. Life after death is a very popular belief. Different cultures view the after-life in a variety of ways. Some embrace it, some fear it, and some foolishly reject it altogether. Life after death is not a new idea; in fact, it's older than dirt. Every religion asks the same questions: what happens after we die, where do we go, what role are we to play, is there really a heaven and a hell? We should consider heaven and what awaits us there. Life here can be very distracting if we're too comfortable. We will neglect thinking about heaven altogether. Be careful, there is imminent danger in procrastination.

If there were evidence proving there is life after death, would you believe it? Could you have doubts of an afterlife, a place beyond this world, if someone had gone there and come back? Even if it could be proved, some people would not embrace it. Deep seated feelings and empirical evidence war against each other. It has been said that a person is only eighteen inches from the Kingdom of God: the distance between his heart and his mind. Will your heart make the emotional decision or will your mind reason it out and make a rational decision?

There is no religious belief, no philosophical reasoning, no intu-ition, no incantation, and certainly no dream, that compares to the plain truth. That someone could come from heaven, live among us, tell us about it, and then return there, is almost beyond belief. If someone did all these things, and then one day, at one appointed time, came back to reclaim us and take us there – would that convince you? Don't just wait and see. Make your decision now. Don't wait for a decisive convergence, or worse, cognitive dissonance. Be reawakened now.

The theory of cognitive dissonance states that contradicting or clashing thoughts cause discomfort. When our thoughts are not consistent, either our behavior or our attitude must change. Dissonance comes when an action *and* an attitude are in conflict. Dissonance can also occur when an action is not justified by the outcome.

People who have to choose between two highly desirable choices will experience a high level of cognitive dissonance. What could be some of those difficult choices? The best example is: Do I do things *my way*, or *God's way*?

The classic illustration in the Bible is when the apostle Paul wrestled with the issue (see Romans 7:15-25). He said: "For what I want to do I do not do...I have the desire to do what is good, but I cannot carry it out...When I want to do good, evil is right there with me...I see another law at work in the members of my body, waging war against the law of my mind... Who will rescue me from this?" This is cognitive dissonance.

We can settle the matter by reading Romans chapter 8. Paraphrased, it says that those who live according to the sinful nature have their minds set on their natural desires, but those who live in accordance with the spirit have their minds set on what the spirit desires. The mind of sinful man is death, but the mind controlled by the spirit is life and peace.

Some of the most comforting words ever found in the Bible are in the Gospel of John. This is the promise Jesus made:

> "Do not let you hearts be troubled.
> Trust in God, trust also in me.
> In my Father's house are many rooms;
> if it were not so, I would have told you.

I am going there to prepare a place for you.
And if I go and prepare a place for you, I will come back
and take you to be with me that you also
may be where I am."
John 14:1-3

These words offer hope, assurance, and a promise of an afterlife. Jesus told us in His own words how we get to God:

"I am the way and the truth and the life.
No one comes to the Father except through me."
John 14:6

Christians believe that there is only one way to heaven. This belief troubles many people because lots of them say, "We're all going to the same destination – we're just taking different paths." Other people merely parrot the phrase, "It doesn't matter what you believe in, just as long as you're sincere". Wrong and double wrong! The fact is, the truth has always been the narrow way. Sincerity is important, but it has never been a substitute for the truth. Christians didn't just make this up. Jesus Himself said that He was the *only* way, and proved His authority by the resurrection. You can thank God that there *is* a way!

"Salvation is found in no one else,
for there is no other name under heaven
given to men by which we must be saved."
Acts 4:12

"Enter through the narrow gate.
For wide is the gate and broad is the road
that leads to destruction, and *many* enter through it.
But small is the gate and narrow the road that leads to life,
and only a *few* find it."(emphasis added)
Matthew 7:13-14

Matthew chapter 14 gives us a narrow-gate warning. There is one way to heaven, not many. Christianity is exclusive. There is no room for diversity. There is no room for multiculturalism. There is no room for error. It is on God's terms, and God's way: the narrow road.

There are various cultural identities about heaven and it means something different to each belief. Most religions have some teachings on life after death. For the followers of Islam, heaven is compared to a harem of carnal lust. The Buddhists' image of heaven is nirvana – nothingness; a sense of being unmoved and unaware of anything except mere existence. Hindus live repeatedly through reincarnation, again and again and yet again. In these examples, there is no hope of God's presence. There is no freedom from the consequences of sin. There is no reconciliation with our creator. Where are our loved ones who have died, and where is that lost Garden of Eden that God intended?

What do Christians believe about life after death? Christians believe that life goes only one way, not in circles. We pass through death only one time, and what happens *beyond* this life depends heavily on what happens *in* this life. It is here that Christianity is separated from other religions. Generally, religion tries to get people to make themselves good enough for a positive afterlife. Christianity says simply: it can't be done! You cannot buy, bribe, sneak, nor work your way into heaven. Jesus has already paid the price for your admission. It is by grace, through faith, or not at all (see Ephesians 2:8-9).

The Bible points out that by the time we know that we are sinners, we are drowning in sin. Religion screams at those drowning, "swim harder"! Christianity offers to rescue that person by sending a lifeguard, a Savior - Jesus Christ.

"But God demonstrates his own love for us in this:
While we were still sinners, Christ died for us."
Romans 5:8

The Christian faith has one who came from heaven and conquered death, hell, and the grave. He has plans for those who believe in Him to join Him in His heavenly realm. It is a physical place, not a state of mind, an idea, wishful thinking, or a figure of speech. It is not a sentiment, a feeling, or an emotion. It is a holy place where God dwells and there is no presence of evil. It is a place of beauty, of completeness, of infinity. Religion is humanity reaching out to a god, any god. Christianity is *the One God* reaching out to a lost humanity. The difference between life and death is religion. The difference between heaven and the place of torments is Christianity.

For the Christian, your citizenship is in heaven (see Philippians 3:20), your name is written in heaven (see Luke 10:20), and your treasures are safely stored in heaven (see Matthew 6:20). For the Christian, your home is being prepared for you in heaven, awaiting your arrival (see John 14:2).

The patriarchs will be there: Abraham, Isaac, Jacob, and Joseph. The beggar at the rich man's gate will be there (see Luke 16:22). The repentant thief who died beside Christ will be there also (see Luke 23:43). All the writers of the Old Testament will be there: Moses, Isaiah, Daniel, Jonah and others. All the writers of the New Testament will be there, including Matthew, Mark, Luke, John, Peter, Paul, and James. Only there can you talk with the writers personally and discuss their walk with God. It will be an awesome gathering of history's faithful in God's house. You don't want to miss it for the world.

Jesus stressed to the religious leaders of his day that it was critical to understand God and His power rather than worry about what heaven would be like. Every generation models their idea of heaven based on their beliefs, desires, and experiences. Jesus told them this was *idle thinking*. You cannot make up your own ideas of heaven and God based on human reasoning. Christ stressed that we should instead concentrate on our relationship with God. Our understanding and appreciation of God will come as needed.

Have you been focusing on making yourself comfortable with the ways of the world? This is not your home! It never has been and it never will be. God will create a new heaven and a new earth (see Revelation 21:1, Isaiah 65:17), where we will live with our creator forever. The Holy Spirit will instruct and guide and comfort us until we are called home. At the present we can only see a poor reflection as in a mirror, but later we will see God face to face. Until that happens, all your worrying is for nothing. God only asks that we trust and obey.

The injustice of this life cries out for another creation, one untouched by sin. God is making the necessary preparations. He would not abandon us to a predator in a sinful universe. There is moral law with a righteous judge that demands an adjustment after life on earth. God takes His responsibilities seriously. He has never, ever failed on His promises.

We place status, wealth, looks, power, and education on pedestals, but Christ said that the least among you will be the greatest. What does that mean? It means the proud, the arrogant, and the haughty will be alienated because they alienated themselves. Christ valued humility and servanthood and unselfishness. God entered *our* world and died for us, so that we can enter *His* world and commune with Him. Try to picture His world - a world without spot or blemish, a world reminiscent of the garden, a world absent the seven deadly sins: a world absent *any* sin. It will truly be "out of this world!" It will be incomprehensible. It will be *just for you*.

God's new kingdom will not be a mere extension of this life. The same natural and physical rules won't apply. However, God's covenant with His followers exists and extends beyond common death. Jesus said He is preparing a place for us. The transportation to get there has already been settled and the destination reserved. The only issue you must settle, before your death, is whether you believe His plan of salvation or not, and have accepted Him as your Lord and Savior.

God has amazing plans for those who love Him. If we learn to love and trust God now, we won't be afraid when we're ushered into His presence later. We should not live so carelessly that when we meet our creator, we have a surprised look on our face. Mediocrity is unacceptable. A Christian has an obligation to be a disciple in every area of his life. Jesus said, "If anyone is ashamed of me and my words in this adulterous and sinful generation, the son of Man will be ashamed of him when he comes in his Father's glory with the holy angels." (Mark 8:38)

If you do not believe God and His plan for your salvation, then what do you believe? Can you put it into words? Can you write it down and explain it to others? Can you trust your very life on it? Where is the wellspring of your hope and your source of authority? For the Christian, proof of the redemption is but one of the sources of our faith. Only those who believe God wholeheartedly know that Jesus is the only way to heaven. Your belief becomes something you are because Christ becomes part of you.

In the book of Acts, the apostle Paul addressed a group concerning an altar they had erected. There were altars to every god they knew including an altar to *the unknown god*. The people of Athens didn't want to miss any god. They were searching for God even in their ignorance. Paul introduced them to the one true God in Acts 17:22-31.

The book of Revelation was written by John the Apostle, better known as John the Revelator. He describes glimpses of heaven for us that he witnessed. God showed him portions of the glory and splendor of heaven to comfort us in our fear of the unknown. Christ told John to record the things he was about to see *in the Spirit* - not with human eyes, but by divine revelation (see Revelation 1:9-11). John was the only one given this special insight, and then told to record it for history in the generations to come.

In heaven you will be given the full understanding of Christ's sacrifice. You will see things as they really are, free from sin's illusions. You have special gifts and talents you will never fully use on earth. They could be called into service in heaven. The grave will not hold all the treasures God has put within you. Your occupation in heaven shouldn't worry you. The presence of the Lord will overshadow any preoccupation with ourselves.

The world we live in is constantly and unpredictably changing. We can learn to live in this world, no matter how perplexing it becomes, but we were created for more - we were created for heaven. Before you die, make sure you're traveling that narrow road. Prepare to live in a world made by God, a world created through the powers of truth and love. It will be a world with no corruption, no terror, and no worry. It will be a place free of loneliness, despair, and disease. In God's world, there is no temptation, no tempter, and no death.

Could you find peace and joy and contentment in a celestial world that had no sin? A world where there was no darkness, nothing sinister, and not even a hint of impurity? A world where there were no hospital waiting rooms, no depression, and no chemotherapy? There will be a heavenly world where God is sovereign, and we will be there because we accepted an invitation – not because of any birthright, work, chance, or serendipity.

You were created to be a citizen of heaven, not a prisoner of sin. God invested Himself in you, and He is coming back to reclaim what is His. Your battle is not with people, but with invisible forces. Jesus is the only one who conquered sin and can show us the road to paradise. Idol/idle time is the devil's scheme. Satan does not want you to have an afterlife; he wants you to be consumed by sin. He wants you to ignore God's word. He wants you to delay and procrastinate. He wants you to quit seeking that narrow path to life everlasting.

> "We fix our eyes not on what is seen,
> but on what is unseen.
> For what is seen is temporary,
> but what is unseen is eternal."
> 2 Corinthians 4:18

The Bible tells us to resist the devil, and stand firm in the faith of Christ (see 1 Peter 5:9). We should direct our attention to heaven and to Him who dwells there. The world did not learn about God through its own wisdom (see 2 Corinthians 1:21).

Do you want to be happy, strong, and joyous? Set aside a quiet time to really think about heaven. The Bible says we should ponder it! No one can even imagine what awaits those who earnestly yearn for God's presence.

> "Eye hath not seen,
> nor ear heard,
> neither have entered into the heart of man,
> the things which God hath prepared
> for them that love him."
> 1 Corinthians 2:9 KJV

Christ didn't fight the people who drove nails into His hands. He looked beyond that. He looked to please the Father. He looked to those without hope – He looked at you. He fixed His eyes squarely on heaven. He is there now, waiting to roll out the red carpet. Christ is seeking you for His kingdom, but you must make yourself available to be found. Seek the narrow path. Send up a homing beacon; send up a prayer of repentance. He will recognize you. After all, you are just trying to get back to where you came from. Christ is calling you to come back. He was, and still is, all about you.

Chapter 9

Angels Among Us

People all over the world believe in angels. Do you? What kind of angels do you believe in? Good ones, bad ones? The Scriptures speak volumes about them. Angels profoundly affect our peace and safety as we journey through this world. Angels and demons attend our very steps – some as kind ministering spirits, some to murder us in body and soul. They play a panorama of roles in our lives, but only those roles the creator desires. These supernatural beings are altering our very history.

Angels concentrate on the hands-on aspect of heavenly service, while the Holy Spirit applies Himself to the ministry of our inner self. We need to be reminded that the term *angel* designates an office, an official position, a courtier to the King of kings. The word angel, when not qualified by circumstances, simply means *messenger*.

Down through the ages the questions have remained the same. Where are angels from? Where do they live? Are they people who have died? What role do they play on earth, and in heaven? Are they reclined on billowy clouds playing harps of gold? Scripture has numerous passages that tell us heaven - not earth - is their place of residence. Isaiah 6:1-6 portrays angels attending God's throne in heaven. Daniel 7:10 pictures *thousands upon thousands,* and *ten thousand times ten thousand* before God. Second Chronicles 18:18 puts the Lord on His throne and all the host of heaven on His right and on His left. In John 1:51, Jesus speaks of angels ascending and descending to and from heaven.

They live and work where God decides they live and work. Their assigned tasks take them to and from heaven and all points in between. The *function* of an angel is as a messenger, even though it is not the *nature* of an angel.

Angels have distinct personalities. They possess a highly refined intellect (see 1 Peter 1:12), display a range and intensity of emotions (see Luke 2:13-14), can exercise sovereign will (see Jude 6), possess great power (see 2 Peter 2:11), and were created to be distinct from human beings (see Psalms 8:3-5). They have many of the qualities we were created with, but unlike us, they do not marry, procreate, or die (see Mark 12:25; Luke 20:36). Their ranks haven't been increased by marriage nor decreased by death.

The characteristics of angels have two distinct orders: those that are holy and good and those that are evil. They were not always segregated. At one point in the twilight of creation all angels were created perfect and holy. Each of them, like you, possessed a moral liberty of free will. When tested, some angels, "Kept not their first estate [place]" (Jude 6), a position of rank and holiness. They rebelled against God their creator. Lucifer, the instigator and leader, better known as the morning star, encouraged others to rebel with him against God. The result was chaos in the heavenly realms. A third of the angels created were found contaminated with sin and expelled from God's heaven. They were banished because the presence of evil cannot dwell in the presence of the Almighty God.

Angels are incredibly diverse and can be awesome in appearance. They can appear like fellow travelers on the road (see Genesis 19:1), or be like ourselves and touch us as flesh to flesh (see Daniel 10:18). Angels have been seen and described by many notable people. The cherubim angels Ezekiel saw had wings (see Ezekiel 1:6). The seraphim angels described by Isaiah also had wings, and were flying, and were speaking to each other (see Isaiah 6:1-5).

Daniel's friends stood shaking at the sound of an angel's voice. Zechariah was unable to speak by the authority of an angel's word. At the birth of the Messiah, even the lowly shepherds were awed by their presence and glory. Angels ate food with Abraham; led

Lot and his family out of Sodom; and Mary, the mother of Jesus, had a conversation with an angel named Gabriel. Mary's husband Joseph was told by an angel that her child was to be named Jesus. All conveyed an important message.

Scripture clearly shows that angels were created by God to be His ambassadors, His representatives, His messengers. Christ knew about and taught the existence of angels (see Matthew 18:10; 26:53), their numbers (see Hebrews 12:22), their power (see 2 Kings 19:35), and their place about the throne of God (see Revelation 5:11; 7:11). Their relationship to Christians is that of *ministering spirits* (see Daniel 6:22; Matthew 2:13,19,20; Luke 22:43; Acts 5:19, 12:7-10). The angels also observe our lives (see 1 Corinthians 4:9), a gentle reminder that should influence our present conduct.

Scripture says that man was made a little lower than the angels, and Christ took upon Himself this position, that eventually He might lift the Christian into the sphere above angels (see Hebrews 2:9-10). It is the angels who will accompany Christ in His second advent (see Matthew 25:31). The angels are commissioned to prepare for the judgment of individual Gentiles among the nations (see Matthew 13:36-43; 25:31-32).

The archangel Michael has a special relationship with the nation Israel and to the resurrection (see Daniel 10:13-21; 12:1-2; 1 Thessalonians 4:16). The only other angel whose name is revealed, Gabriel, had some very distinguished appointments (see Daniel 8:15-17; 9:20-27; Luke 1:19, 26-38). Other angels, yet unnamed, have positions of authority and are given awesome tasks to be performed at the end of this age, some so terrifying only God can restrain (see Revelation 8-9).

Regarding fallen angels, two types are mentioned in Scripture: [1] The angels who rebelled with Satan and are chained under darkness, awaiting judgment (see Jude 6; 2 Peter 2:4; 1 Corinthians 6:3), and [2] the angels who are not bound but still free, and doing the will of Satan.

After being cast out of heaven, Satan and his followers have waged war against the work of God on behalf of humanity. His work against God continues. Given strictly limited power, he is considered the "Prince of the power of the air" (see Ephesians 2:2 KJV).

Although he is the prince of this present world system, Satan's access to God will end soon. After the Second Coming of Christ, he will be bound for a thousand years (see Revelation 20:2), released for a short time (see Revelation 20:3-8), then ultimately judged and cast into the lake of fire - his final punishment.

When studying medicine to become physicians, the prime directive in the Hippocratic oath is "First do no harm". The study of angels also has a similar directive, "Rightly divide the Word of Truth". We are not to deceive or be deceived. We are to compare Scripture to Scripture. Second Timothy 2:15 says that we are to study the Scriptures to show ourselves approved. We are to compare and contrast the Scripture, in both analysis and presentation. Be prepared to share and defend your faith. You can believe what your parents and grandparents believed, but unless you know *what you* believe, and *why you* believe it, you can be fed lies just as Eve was in the Garden of Eden.

Angelology is the methodical approach to the study of angels: their existence, creation, personality, nature, and their work. It extends to their intellect, emotions, will, and service to their creator. There is a hierarchy of angels from the Archangel Michael to guardian angels (for all, see Hebrews 1:14; for children, see Matthew 18:10). Scripture reveals to us there are chief princes (see Daniel 10:13), ruling angels (see Ephesians 3:10), and elect angels (see 1 Timothy 5:21).

The duty and role of these angels is only hinted at in Scripture. Some of their positions are delineated. The seraphim (see Isaiah 6:1-3) have to do with the worship of God, while the cherubim (see Genesis 3:22-24) speak of guarding the holiness of God. Revelation 5:11 speaks of angels by the millions, so it is obvious these few examples are only a hint of their positions of influence.

Angels once played only a limited role in our lives. They showed up on Christmas cards, in popular songs, and occasionally played a part in movies. But lately there's been a powerful shift in our Western culture. Angels have moved from myth to metaphor to mainstream. Books and magazines are rife with stories of angels and their exploits. Even the amoral Hollywood has discovered, "Thar's gold in them thar hills!" In short, angels are big business!

Hollywood has declared that angels should be treated as a commodity. How many popular movies and television series portray angels in them? Warning of unseen danger, protecting little children, rescuing humanity, fighting evil – they're seen as all-knowing and all-powerful, being everywhere at once. Like the crafty serpent in the Garden of Eden, these examples of angels are perfectly good half-lies. The truth is that only God can be everywhere. Omnipresence is one of His attributes.

But what is real and what's counterfeit? Hebrews 1:14 asks, "Are not all angels ministering spirits sent to serve those who will inherit salvation?" That is an excellent question. Perhaps the answer is found in the next verse, Hebrews 2:1, which says, "We must pay more careful attention, therefore, to what we have heard, so that we do not drift away."

We are inundated with angelmania: the irrational, unscriptural, touchy-feely position that anything having to do with angels must be good, exciting, and helpful. The popularity of angels is increasing exponentially. But why is angelmania the current craze in North America? This growing fascination is proving to be a popular diversion without any theological basis or serious consideration. It appears to be all smoke and mirrors, and precious little substance.

This unhealthy preoccupation with angels is a game of spiritual flirting. It is religiosity without reading the Bible to learn about truth firsthand. America has an unquenchable thirst for angels and how they relate to our lives. Christians are comfortable with angels because it is an established biblical doctrine. Others are excited about angels because the world paints a non-Biblical portrait, stirring up our emotional feelings instead of our cognitive facilities.

We seek guardian angels to comfort us in our own insecurities such as homelessness, world hunger, crime, and pollution. We desire angels to somehow make our daily problems more manageable and help us deal with our uncertainty. Maybe the reason we don't find God is that we're seeking a substitute.

The world is selfish and unconcerned about your troubles. We are a gullible generation. We desire that angels somehow intervene in our lives and bring us closer to God through their association with

Him. Angels can intervene in our lives, and they have appeared to people, and it's almost always unexpected. People who have been confronted by angels have all had a similar response – fear. God's reply was the same to everyone – do not be afraid. After their fear subsided, they felt God's presence; then God could communicate His message to them. God released them from their fears so they could draw close to Him. He gives you the same freedom. Everyone feels fear, but do not let it stop you from seeking God. "The fear of the Lord is the beginning of wisdom" (Psalm 111:10).

People search for God in creative ways. Some create idols, some worship nature, and others seek angels as a substitute. The need to be united with our creator is universal. Everyone has that longing to know God. The questions we have are primal. Who am I, why am I here, what's my purpose in life? The philosopher Blaise Pascal once said, "There's a God-shaped vacuum in the center of every human heart." Jesus Christ came to fill that vacuum so that we may know God's love for us and never be lost and alone again.

Most of the angel craze infecting America has little to do with the heavenly hosts described in the Bible. Most of the fanfare would have more in common with *fallen* angels than with *holy* angels. If they create spirituality without Christ and without God, they are false and unholy imposters.

> "And no wonder, for Satan himself masquerades
> as an angel of light. It is not surprising, then,
> if his servants masquerade as servants of righteousness.
> Their end will be what their actions deserve."
> 2 Corinthians 11:14-15

People look for God in angels. They want a personal experience, enlightenment, or a supernatural power to inspire them. With angels, people feel they can receive God's help without dealing directly with God. But angels are not intermediaries to reach God; only Jesus serves that purpose. First Timothy 2:5-6 reminds us, "For there is one God and one mediator between God and men, the man Christ Jesus, who gave himself as a ransom for all men."

Angels are so popular because they offer people of all faiths a spirituality without any commitment to God; a religious approach that offers the seeker a noncommittal, nonjudgmental, and nonthreatening approach to God. Religion-Lite! The traditional Judeo-Christian image of God is too strict for some. They want a God filled with love without any hint of wrath or shed blood. Angels are a perfect compromise, like soft cuddly teddy bears; there is one to fit every situation. Just look at the advantages offered; they are seen as utterly compassionate, temptation-free, protective, always accessible, and politically correct.

Angels are more popular than ever because the world thinks they are helping people. But how? Are they helping us to cope with uncertainty, pain, and suffering? Do they offer a hedge of protection in a world threatened on all sides? Do we need angels more than ever? Do we need angels to bridge a gateway to a higher consciousness? Why is this desire to connect with angels so strong?

Materialism does not satisfy, and science and technology haven't gotten us any closer to God. Why not grasp for angels? They make us feel good - we hope and believe they will provide us with happiness, health, wealth, romance, success - they can even double as good luck charms. That, however, is merely trying to replace God with something much less valuable.

Angelmania is fascinating to this generation. While it may strike a chord deep within all of us, it cheapens the image of those heavenly beings. Does the grim image of God's angels destroying the cities of Sodom and Gomorrah remind you of soft cuddly teddy bears or of the Creator sending a warning? There are angel boutiques, angel calendars, angel coffee mugs, angel refrigerator magnets, limited edition porcelain angel collectibles, etc. etc. ... *ad nauseam*. There is also the image of an angel wielding a flaming sword preventing Adam and Eve from returning to the Garden of Eden!

Angels have mostly served as a peaceful example of power deferred, but on occasion, their awesome power is released. Jesus often spoke in parables while teaching. In Matthew, chapter 13, Jesus told how the kingdom of heaven was like a great dragnet that was lowered into a lake and when pulled up caught all manner of fish. He further explained that the lake represented the world and that the fish represented people, both the righteous and the wicked. He said that the angels would separate them, some to keep and some to discard. *Why* these angels were given this enormous task was on command from heaven. *How* this task is to be carried out is not for us to know.

Scriptures show us that angels are generally *incorporeal,* lacking material form or substance. They may be invisible, but they are not merely impersonal influences. Some of the greatest moments in history were affected by angels, caused by angels, or witnessed by angels. Luke 15:10 tells us that angels rejoice when sinners repent. John 20:12 states there were angels at the tomb of Jesus after His resurrection. Acts 1:10 informs us that angels were present when Jesus ascended to heaven. Don't be confused, there *are* angels among us.

God uses unusual methods to communicate with us. Jacob, Joseph, and the great Pharaoh of Egypt had some very troubling dreams. Belshazzar received a personal letter that just happened to be written on a stone wall – by the very hand of God! Balaam was spoken to by an irate donkey. In the great Exodus, when the Jews left Egypt, the nation of Israel found God directing them to the Promised Land by a pillar of cloud during the day and a pillar of fire by night. Moses had his burning bush in the desert. Saint Peter had his crowing rooster. Saint Paul had his blinding light on the road to Damascus. Job had his losses and his boils.

These men learned that God was in control of their destiny, not angels. We cannot substitute anything or anyone for the God we depend on for our salvation. That God-shaped vacuum can only be filled by Jesus Christ. The Word of God is our only source of truth and life. God used various ways to reach these men, great and small. How is God trying to reach you? Are you reachable?

"Do not forget to entertain strangers, for by so doing some
people have entertained angels without knowing it."
Hebrews 13:2

Who says God does not have a sense of humor? What better way to see if we are living the life we claim than to be put to the angel test. Just as we are trying to be Christlike in an un-Christlike world, God is watching us – at work, at play, at worship. Have you entertained His friends, His messengers, His heavenly hosts? It may be all about angels for now, but one day, it will certainly be all about you!

Chapter 10

Who's Your Shepherd?

We know something about angels, heaven, hell, and the devil. We desire to know more about these mysteries and others as well. We want answers to our oldest questions, but one question often leads to other questions even more fundamental. You are not alone when you question your earthly purpose and your life's journey. We are earnestly yearning for something deeper, something primal. Our very essence is truly thirsting for answers to questions that only God can supply.

These are questions and feelings that God expects us to ponder and ask, and furthermore, He wants us to seek Him for the answers. Are we merely seeking answers to questions or is something deeper troubling us? What we really want to know is – everything about God! How can we know God personally? God already knows us personally and intimately and He desires that we know Him in like manner. Ever since the Garden of Eden we have desired Him. The Psalmist cut to the heart and soul of the matter when he wrote:

"For you created my inmost being;
you knit me together in my mother's womb.
I praise you because I am fearfully and wonderfully made."
Psalm 139:13-14

We want our questions answered; we want to know what God thinks about us. We want what Adam had in the garden, a daily walk and talk with God. We want to know: who is God? what is God like? what has He revealed to us about Himself? what is His will and plan for us? what are His attributes, values, and traits? We have so many questions and yet the answer for each of them is made available to us through His word – the Bible. God *has* revealed Himself to us. He *has* invited us to know Him, through the life and work of His son Jesus. He *has* told us everything we desire to know about Him, through Holy Writ. We are the ones who remain ignorant if we fail to acknowledge what He *has* done for us.

> "Come now, let us reason together,
> says the Lord."
> Isaiah 1:18

People have known about God from the very beginning. Time and time again, the world has rejected God and His ways. Suffering is the consequence. Cause and effect! The world knew God was righteous and full of truth, but instead decided to become wicked and godless. Mankind is condemned because truth was given and the world rejected it. The proof is recorded in Romans:

> "What may be known about God is plain to them,
> because God has made it plain to them.
> For although they knew God, they neither glorified
> him as God nor gave thanks to him."
> Romans 1: 19-21

God created us – we did not create God. After some rejected His creation, His word, and His son, God still reached out and offered an olive branch. Some still spurned God and yet somehow, God continues to call us to learn about Him, promising forgiveness and a place in heaven! Is this a God of vengeance or a God of love? If this is a God we cannot understand, surely it is a God to whom we can give the benefit of doubt.

Even though we know so little, could we, or would we want to, live in a world where God did not exist? What hope would we have? Reincarnation, so we could go in a continuous circle? Fame and fortune, so we could have monuments erected in our honor? Power, so we could have the adoration and approval of men? There is so much to learn about God and time is fleeting.

You must take the initiative and learn about God, because an unknown god cannot be served, worshipped, or even trusted. You need more than a theoretical knowledge of God. We can only truly know God if we yield ourselves to Him, be obedient to His precepts and His commandments, and submit to His ultimate authority. Jesus told His disciples, "If you really knew me, you would know the Father as well" (John 14:7). God has put within all of us a homing beacon, a spirit and soul that always points toward heaven like a compass needle. However, if we ignore it and never use it, we will remain lost in the cosmos.

God has provided everything we need to seek Him, find Him, and ultimately know Him. God has laid everything out for us in plain sight. We must react and reciprocate this generosity. We should not dare to ignore such a gracious invitation. It is imperative for us to discover and learn of Him. God is known as the great I Am, the Alpha and the Omega, the King of kings, and the Lord of all lords. Once we learn the truth, our lives are forever changed - we can never go back into that cave of darkness and ignorance. Jesus came as the sacrificial lamb of God to set us free from sin.

"If we deliberately keep on sinning
after we have received the knowledge of the truth,
no sacrifice for sins is left,
but only a fearful expectation of judgment
and of raging fire that will consume the enemies of God."
Hebrews 10:26-27

To understand God is to accept that God is sovereign, divine, holy, and solitary in His uniqueness. Moses writes early on in the book of Exodus: "Who among the gods is like you, O Lord? Who is like you – majestic in holiness, awesome in glory, working wonders?" (Exodus 15:11). The question is a valid one. Who is like God? The answer is simple, there is none. Down through history there have been a lot of *"small g"* gods, but only one *"big G"* God who made the worlds and everything in them. There is only one God who made you and calls you to return to the one who made you. The prophet Isaiah says that there is only one God who "Makes known the end from the beginning, from ancient times, what is still to come" (Isaiah 46:10).

Isaiah revealed something about God that everyone is curious about. Does God see the future? Of course He can! He sees the past, from the future! God can forecast the future because He knows the sequence of events, the beginning and the end, before they happen. Consider these few examples:

- The Messiah will be born in Bethlehem, Ephrata ... [He was]
- Nebuchadnezzar, tonight, your kingdom will fall ... [It did]
- Jesus said, destroy this temple and I will raise it again in three days [He did]

These examples tell us everything we need to know about God's omniscience. They were for His glory and our benefit. The Bible clearly shows a God of wisdom, strength, and abundant mercy in these examples.

God is sovereign, the Lord of heaven and earth. He is subject to none, and influenced by none. He is independent and indivisible. He is unrivaled in majesty, unlimited in power. He is potentate of everything without and within His creation.

Through His sovereignty, He placed the angels in Heaven, Adam and Eve in the Garden of Eden, the nation of Israel in His land, and kings and armies to complete and fulfill His will. He makes covenants conditional or unconditional. He makes nations rise or fall. He places rulers in authority and drives them out of authority, all to accomplish His perfect will. All creation observes its place under His guidance.

"The Lord does whatever pleases him,
in the heavens and on the earth,
in the seas and all their depths."
Psalm 135:6

Why should we obey Him? We should obey because of who He is and what He has done. He is God – that should be enough. Why should we fear Him? Because even while we were sinners and deserved severe punishment, God showed love and mercy to those who sought Him. What should we do for Him? In the Gospel of John Jesus said, "The work of God is this: to believe in the one he has sent" (John 6:29).

We cannot hide from God. Adam and Eve tried that in the garden. God came looking for them, and found them hiding from Him. Satan is forever trying to get us to push God out of the picture and do things our own way. We must seek *His* perspective. We must acknowledge that God is not just an *ingredient* of life. He is the *source* of life! We need to persist in knowing Him. We need to seek knowledge, understanding, patience, and wisdom. God is generous and gives freely and abundantly.

God is immutable. *Semper Idem* [always the same]. This attribute distinguishes the creator from the creation. God is not subject to change in His being or His attributes; He is perpetually the same. He can know no change because He has no beginning or end. God does not evolve, improve, or deplete. Everything He has ever been, He will remain; neither to rise nor fall. As God explained to Moses at the burning bush: "I AM WHO I AM" (Exodus 3:14). His power is constant, His wisdom undiminished, and His glory undimmed.

"I am the Lord, I change not."
Malachi 3:6 KJV

In these degenerate times, we seldom meditate on the attributes of God. We must train our brain to reach beyond the pale of everyday existence. We must see God as self-contained, self-sufficient, and self-satisfied - in need of nothing. God is under no obligation, no constraint, and no necessity for any purpose. An obvious question you may ask is, "Why did God create anyone in the first place?" Ephesians 1:5 tells us God did it, "According to the good pleasure of His will." He wanted you. You were chosen.

We are treading on high ground as we talk about the attributes of God. God is both honored and dishonored by men: not in His being, but in His character. It is true that God and God's name have received *Glory* by the whole Creation, by providence, and by redemption. We, the created, are enormously fortunate to have been a part of and a witness to this.

> "Known unto God are all his works
> from the beginning of the world."
> Acts 15:18 KJV

The decrees of God are His pleasures or purposes concerning future things. Scripture mentions God's decrees in various passages under different terms. In Ephesians 3:11 we read of God's *eternal purpose*. In Acts 2:23 we are told of God's *determinate council and foreknowledge*. In Romans 8:29 we learn of God's *predestination*. In Ephesians we read the mystery of God's *will*. God's decrees are often called His *counsel* to show that they are the personification of wisdom. The decrees of God relate to things of the future.

God's decrees have properties. Being divine, they are eternal, wise, and free. God's decrees are also absolute and unconditional. We should be thankful that everything is determined by infinite wisdom and goodness. We can rest securely at night because "For from him and through him and to him are all things" (Romans 11:36).

God has a multiplicity of attributes. He is omniscient. He knows everything: the past, the present, and the future; everything active and everything possible. Nothing escapes His attention. Nothing is forgotten by Him, nothing is hidden, nothing is overlooked. Even though He is invisible to us, we are always in His sight. The wicked hate this attribute! They wish there were no witness to their sins, no searcher of their hearts, and no judge of their actions.

There is the foreknowledge of God, the supremacy of God, the sovereignty of God. There is the holiness of God, the power of God, the faithfulness of God. He is good, patient, merciful, full of grace, and longsuffering. There is the God of Love and the God of Wrath.

We can spend our entire lives learning about God and realize that God is unfathomable. All we really need to know about Him is that He loves us more than anything and that He has provided us with all that we'll ever need. He is our provider, sustainer, protector, defender, counselor, and our loving shepherd.

Our God is a God of forgiveness, and forgiveness of sin through grace is the highest compliment He offers to us. There are other courtesies God favors upon us but this one is by far the most magnanimous. This forgiveness is neither free nor unimportant. Forgiveness of sins demands the shedding of blood. Why? Because life is in the blood, and blood enables us to stay alive. Jesus shed His blood – His life – so we would not have to die a spiritual death: a separation from God.

The Bible has much to say about the blood of Christ. It says that we cannot be redeemed without the shedding of blood. That is verified in several Scriptures, including Hebrews 9:22, Leviticus 17:11, and Ephesians 2:13. All of these references explain that blood, and blood alone, is the atoning agent for our sin. Christ's blood brought peace (see Colossians 1:20); it justifies our salvation (see Romans 5:9); it establishes Jesus as our intercessor (see Romans 8:34); and the blood of Christ purifies and cleanses us of *all* our sin (see 1 John 1:7-9).

This is the only reason God forgives our sin. It is made possible only by the shed blood of Christ. Forgiveness is the first step in restoring our relationship with God. We need to admit our need for forgiveness and accept it when it is offered. Forgiveness will not eliminate the consequences of sin, but it will bring us freedom from guilt. Forgiveness of sin cannot happen without God's mercy – it is an undeserved privilege. It is what brought God the most personal pain and heartache *and* the most personal satisfaction.

The kingdom of God is fast approaching. We are in the very shadow of the end times. What is your disposition? Are you following God, or a form of godliness? You cannot shape God to your own liking - God created you, and one day you will return to Him.

Forgiveness is found only through faith in Christ. You need the forgiveness of sin that only God can offer. You do not want to die in your sins without God. The time to decide is now, while you are holding this book. The Bible says, "now is the day of salvation!" (2 Corinthians 6:2). This is *your* critical time of decision. Is it all about God, or is it all about you?

Chapter 11

Men of Tomorrow

W hen you were a child what did you desire to be when you grew up? A princess, a soldier? Maybe you yearned to be a movie star; rich and famous. Maybe you wanted to be a sports star known the world over. When you became older, did your career ideas change? Did you wish to be a successful doctor, lawyer, opera star, maybe the owner of your own business? Did you actively seek a career, or did you patiently wait for whatever came your way?

Perhaps you didn't have lofty ambitions, but simply wanted to be like your parents. Most people just want to be comfortable, happy, and settled. An average life without fame or fortune pleases most. A life that by any measuring stick would be, well…ordinary. There is a lot to be said for ordinary; after all, that is what most of us are in the beginning, then we change.

Dwight L. Moody, Jim Elliot, Mother Teresa, and Billy Graham all started out with humble beginnings. Simple beginnings maybe, but the providential hand of God led them to have an enormous impact on the world. Few people who started out great have been used by God. Just look at the apostles Jesus picked: a tax collector, a zealot, some fishermen. How do you change the world with average people, those with common trades, individuals who are completely and totally ordinary?

God is not looking for those who are already famous so He can gain the maximum advantage. God looks at those who have the right *heart*, so He can help them grow into what He has already planned for them. Man or woman, young or old, common or royalty, none of that matters; it's in the heart. We can't see it, but God can and does. God gently navigates that individual to seek His will and accomplish His purpose – to become the men of tomorrow.

> "The Lord does not look at the things man looks at.
> Man looks at the outward appearance,
> but the Lord looks at the heart."
> 2 Samuel 16:7

There is a marked contrast between the human and divine perspectives. We only bother with the physical aspects; we would never think that what's on the inside counts more than general appearance. But God looks at our intents, our attitude, and our willingness to become a servant. The Lord told Isaiah, "For my thoughts are not your thoughts, neither are your ways my ways" (Isaiah 55:8).

We are made in God's image. This little fact is what separates us from the animal kingdom. We have reason, morality, and self-worth. When we interact with others we are exchanging traits with beings made in the image of God. Looking past the veneer, we can recognize God's image in all people. God intended for us to see Him in other people and for other people to see Him in us!

The omniscience of God is working in your life whether you become a princess or a soldier; He desires to work in you and through you to touch others. You were formed out of the dust of the ground, a lifeless shell until God breathed into you His *breath of life*. When God removes His life-giving breath, your body will return to dust. Your worth as a human being does not come from your profession or from your accomplishments, but from God who graciously chose to share with you the gift of life.

Most people think that life consists of fulfilling all our appetites. Eat the best foods, dress in the latest fashion, accumulate the latest toys and then live the *good life*. When Jesus was tempted by the devil after fasting (see Matthew 4:4), He quoted Deuteronomy 8:3, "Man does not live on bread alone but on every word that comes from the mouth of the Lord." It takes maturity to realize that material things fail to satisfy our deepest longings. Satan uses materialism to distract and delay our search for God. In the end, it is true - *things* leave us empty and disillusioned.

The only way to enjoy real life is in commitment to God; the One who created life itself. Make no mistake, Jesus said, "But small is the gate and narrow the road that leads to life, and only a few find it" (Matthew 7:14). The journey to total commitment to God is not an easy one to make. Do not be discouraged too easily. Total commitment is not pain free; it requires discipline, sacrifice, hard work, and a willing heart. That is why most people never find it! Only through real effort can our relationship with God deepen, our character be strengthened, our peace of mind be assured, and a deep abiding satisfaction take place. Life is rich and full through total commitment to God.

God is the source of life, and of life everlasting. Life is short no matter how many years you live. If there is something urgent for you to do, don't put it off until tomorrow. The apostle Paul warned those Corinthians who procrastinated, "I tell you, now is the time of God's favor, now is the day of salvation" (2 Corinthians 6:2). Paul's emphasis was on the present; now – today! The brevity of life is portrayed clearly in Psalms and Proverbs. Accumulating a storehouse of riches will carry no weight concerning eternity. Life on earth is temporary; do not be easily fooled by everything shiny and new. As the old saying goes: "Only one life; will soon be past; only what's done for Christ will last".

Realizing that our time is short and life is limited, shouldn't we be focused on things eternal? The Bible says our days are numbered. Only God knows the length and breadth of our lives. Have you ever asked yourself, "What do I want to accomplish in life before I die?" Should you be focused on threescore and ten years, or pleasing God and storing up riches in heaven? God gave you a desire for eternal life; don't be so preoccupied with *this* life that you miss the *other* life. Christ calls you to a higher responsibility than merely finding peace and comfort in this life. To take up your cross and follow Christ means publicly identifying with Him, facing opposition because of Him, even facing suffering and persecution for His sake if necessary.

What kind of life style are you living? Has your faith changed the way you live? Did you know that your future is shaped by how you lived your past? The Bible is filled with examples of God's guidelines and expectations for our daily lives.

Have you studied the Book of Proverbs? You should, it's a scorching good read. It is actually worth more than Goliath's weight in gold! The word *Proverb* derives from a Hebrew word meaning *to govern or to rule*. Technically, a proverb is a brief sentence or paragraph that is very concise and conveys a moral truth. Therefore, Proverbs is a compilation of sayings and admonitions that provides wisdom for *governing* our lives. Knowledge and wisdom are good things, but knowledge without wisdom is rather useless. We must have the facts [*knowledge*] and know how to apply those facts [*wisdom*] to our daily lives in order to please God.

Proverbs is an everyman's guide to practical insights and guidelines for every imaginable facet in life. The overall theme of the Book of Proverbs is the nature of true wisdom and how it applies to your life. The wisest man who ever lived, Solomon, wrote most of the book of Proverbs. God in His infinite wisdom has preserved and protected the Holy Bible so you may learn from the ancients.

Proverbs covers every topic imaginable, from knowing God, seeking the truth, wealth and poverty, youth and old age to marriage and business matters, family life, and resisting temptation. Covering immorality to self-control, it is a treasure trove of Godly wisdom for living your life. The entire Bible is a blueprint for living by God's rules. The Book of Proverbs gives you the finer details of those plans.

It's like having a friend who can help you and give you wise advice your whole life. You have that and more in the Book of Proverbs. Have you ever faced any of these challenges in your life: struggled in school, had jobs or bosses try your patience, marital problems, raised children, faced bankruptcy, or had your health fail?

These are serious personal issues that most people have already faced or may face. But what about matters more intimate, the ones that reach deeper and shake our foundations? There are harder choices that life forces us to absorb and live with day by day. The dire choices, the ones that summon up all your faith; what do you rely on when these situations arise?

- Ever lost your job and had to live on the street?
- Cared for an elderly parent with Alzheimer's?
- Lost a child or a spouse to death?
- Faced life as a quadriplegic?
- Raised a child with severe disabilities?
- Faced hospital bills you couldn't possibly pay?
- Battled an addiction to drugs, alcohol, or gambling?

Most of us ask God, "Why are all these things happening to me?", and then seek the answers in the world. Although more severe, these issues have been faced and overcome through faith in Christ.

"I can do everything through him who gives me strength."
Philippians 4:13

Life is hard, not easy: even unbearable sometimes. Life is unfair and unapologetic. Without hope, life would be pure misery. We are not talking about hope as in good luck, and not the false hope that comes from reading your horoscope. Christian hope is real and it is progressive. It is for today and everlasting. It is a perspective that is reassuring and balanced. Christian hope waits for the promised return of Christ. It makes us the men of tomorrow – God's working people.

We are talking about hope from our creator. Hope from the One who never distorts or disappoints. People can be your best friends for many years, but they can let you down. This is a sad fact about the human condition. Some of the deepest theology is found in a children's song; "Jesus loves me, this I know, for the Bible tells me so". Put your hope in Jesus, He will never let you down.

"A faith and knowledge resting on the hope
of eternal life, which God, who does not lie,
promised before the beginning of time."
Titus 1:2

Have you become enamored with your physical condition rather than your spiritual condition, gathering up earthly mementoes to cherish and neglecting the kingdom of God? Remember the nation of Israel in its early years: they suffered cruelly under the Egyptians for over four hundred years! But when God delivered them in the great Exodus, they witnessed spectacular miracles from God: the ten plagues that broke Pharaoh's spirit, crossing the Red Sea on dry ground, watching the sea engulf the Egyptian army and destroy them! Imagine God leading the entire nation of millions by a pillar of cloud by day and by a pillar of fire by night. The Passover is still celebrated centuries later as a memorial to a living God!

Even though God provided for the Israelites, they still murmured, complained, and rebelled. We wonder how they could be so callous and indifferent – so blind to all God had done for them, but we repeat the same pattern. We've had centuries of watching God working miracles, seeing the Bible printed in every major language, archeological proofs that the Bible is accurate in every detail. Still, people ignore and disobey God and follow idols, seek false gods, and yearn to go their own way. Like the Israelites thirty-five hundred years ago, we put priority on our physical condition rather than our spiritual condition.

The only way to escape this pattern of behavior is to focus your attention on God's presence: the prayers He has answered, the dangers He has kept from you, and the blessings He has showered upon you. Have you never felt His guidance, His protection, His healings, and His incredible patience with your rebellion? Of course you have! Now it's time to focus on your spiritual condition.

If you desire to change for the better, quit delaying - take action and change your mind, your behavior, and your belief. Start putting God at the forefront of your decisions. If your life isn't the way you want it to be, don't assume it will be easier to change it later. The older we get the harder change comes to us. A life of inconsistency, disobedience, and self-will can only end in disaster. Face life the way you want to face death: dependent on God, resolute in His promises, faithful to the very end.

Stop living a life controlled by your affections, your greed, and your selfish interests. You can adjust to the culture without compromising your values. Jesus did it every day of His life, and still sets the example for today. God's way of living contradicts the ways of the world. In the Sermon on the Mount in Matthew, Jesus told how to be happy or blessed, not how to get pleasure, or laughter, or prosperity. Jesus taught how to obtain joy and hope – regardless of your circumstances. In the kingdom of God, wealth, power, and authority are unimportant. God rules, not man. The old order will pass away.

How are we supposed to live until Christ returns? Jesus gave us several parables as lessons. In the parable of the bridesmaids, (see Matthew 25:1-13) we learn that everyone is responsible for his own spiritual condition. The parable of the talents, (see vv. 14-30) teaches us to use wisely what God entrusts to us. The parable of the sheep and goats, (see vv. 31-46) reminds us of the value of serving others in need.

Whatever your past contains, Jesus Christ can provide the comfort and peace you need. You can have a new life awaiting you in God's kingdom. Your present lifestyle is an advertisement. Can people see God in your actions? What do people think from observing your life? Are you telling others how to behave, and then misbehaving yourself? Do you find it easier to give out advice, and ignore it yourself? If you claim to be a Christian, your life should match what Christ is like. Take care that your actions match your words. Your lifestyle is an advertisement, remember? Are you drawing people to God, or representing God by false advertising?

Life is not a rehearsal for a play. It is real. Now is the time to decide whether or not you believe God and the Bible. Then live out your life based on what you decide. God will examine your life in detail. Be consistent and diligent in your approach to life. Read the Bible, seek God's will, build His word into your life. Life already has enough spectators: so get off that fence, and be a participant! Seek to do the works that please God and serve His causes.

When Jesus returns you need to be ready. Preparation is everything. Athletes and soldiers have a saying, "stay ready – don't get ready". Be prepared at all times and don't panic at the moment faith is needed. When the time comes, your relationship with God must be your own. *Wholly* your own. You cannot borrow or buy favors that do not exist. You can believe what your parents believed, your grandparents, even your great-grandparents, but when facing God, you stand alone. When it's all about you, you will have to explain and defend your beliefs about Jesus Christ.

Life lessons to fill a lifetime are contained in the Bible. The first two children born to Adam and Eve were the brothers Cain and Abel. One day both offered gifts to God. One offered choice fruits and vegetables, the other offered the firstborn of his flocks. God was pleased with one's offering and displeased with the other's. Because his offering was rejected, Cain became jealous and killed his brother Abel. At the time the whole affair was a mystery. Why would anyone murder another human being? What would incite a brother to kill his own flesh and blood?

God was pleased by Abel's offering because, "by faith Abel offered God a better sacrifice than Cain did" (Hebrews 11:4). Cain's offering may have taken longer to produce, required more labor and sweat, and been the best he could produce. It did not matter, the fact remained – God was not pleased. Rather than making another offering or asking God why it was unacceptable, or even asking his brother for some of his flocks, Cain swelled up with pride and killed his brother! Cain's offering wasn't by faith, it was through obligation. It wasn't from the heart, it was a brotherly competition. Cain wasn't interested in finding out what pleased God; he desired to *replace* an offering by faith with human works.

Be careful you don't follow in Cain's footsteps. Do not be fooled, God is not mocked, tricked, or deceived. Abel was recognized for his obedience and faith, and God was pleased by that combination. Cain, on the other hand, was angry and unrepentant. God saw Cain's heart was becoming hard and bitter, so He exiled him. Adam and Eve must have been heartbroken to see such behavior. No doubt they recalled that they had sinned against God and brought sin to all mankind. Although Cain committed the first murder, he took the sin issue a step further. He had sinned against both God *and* man. This is the first time we see the effects of sin both increasing and becoming worse.

God judges all sins, and because He is just, the punishment is appropriate. God's correction is not out of malice or anger, but to set guidelines for godly living. Left to ourselves, the evil we are capable of is unlimited. God acts as a loving parent, correcting the bad behavior early on so maturity and faith can develop and bring out good works. Like Abel, what we offer to God through our daily lives needs to come by faith from the deepest recesses of our heart. God listens to those who come to Him.

God is faithful to those who obey Him. Obedience is not a sometimes thing, but involves a long-term commitment. It is a daily walk. It is a meeting of the minds. Even though we face daily failures, God responds to our faith. The providence of God always makes the best use of our mistakes. God is not looking for someone trying to be perfect; He looks for those who fall down, pick themselves back up, learn from their mistake, seek forgiveness, and continue to grow in grace. God is looking for persistence and faithful obedience. God's plans are larger than people and their foibles.

Your life and everything in it is an offering to God. Are you offering up a life of servanthood? We are responsible for our actions. With the help of God, any situation can be turned around and become a life changing event. It can be a teachable moment if we're responsive. Sin can and does have some deadly consequences. The results or even the punishment might not show up immediately, but they certainly will come. God has done some of His best work through sinful people. And many times, our lives and works live on beyond us. The writer of Hebrews reminds us of Abel:

> "And by faith he [Abel] still speaks,
> even though he is dead."
> Hebrews 11:4

Hebrews chapter 11 is often referred to as "faith's hall of fame". It shows examples of lives that pleased God, and *continue* to please Him. These individuals not only showed faith and courage, they had the words and actions to show their allegiance to God. Are you really asked to suffer for God or the name of Christ? In the United States, it is unlikely. There is little danger of becoming a martyr, being imprisoned for life, or facing execution because of your beliefs. That may change in the future, but for the present we are, without doubt, a most God-blessed nation.

It has never been easier, safer, or freer to be a Christian in this country. Our present challenges and responsibilities are trifles compared to some missionaries in other countries. It is entirely possible that God may see our discontentment and grumblings and start withdrawing His blessings from this nation. We could lose His favor - after all, we have invited Him out of our schools, out of our government buildings, and almost out of our churches. We have taken prayer for granted and pushed our creator aside in favor of self. Remember: God is, and will forever be, ruler of our universe. He has given us a blueprint for generations past and future in Second Chronicles. It speaks volumes about God's requirements for blessings. We need humility, prayer, devotion, and repentance.

"If my people who are called by my name,
will humble themselves and pray and seek my face
and turn from their wicked ways,
then I will hear from heaven and will forgive their sin
and will heal their land."
2 Chronicles 7:14

If His people, who are called by His name, will only repent, God Himself will personally intervene! That is powerful! Bear in mind that God has never broken a promise or failed to keep one He has made. We, on the other hand, cannot say that our fidelity is flawless. This beautiful promise from the book of Chronicles cannot be assured by Buddha, Confucius, Islam, any other cult, or even any other religion. How about from any other deity? Government certainly cannot make that promise and keep even a fraction of it. The Roman Empire could not survive the steady erosion of its moral standards, and neither can America, if we follow in the footsteps of the Roman leaders.

Can you showcase any promise like it from anywhere else? If you can, produce it – chapter and verse - and show that past promises have always been kept, and past prophecies have always been fulfilled, and answers to impossible prayers have been answered. Go ahead, put God to the test. You can read about the one man who earnestly questioned God and God answered him. You will find the account of their conversation in the book of Job.

Obedience results from a relationship with God. God *wants* obedience from the heart. Good works are nice, religious acts are noticed, and helping the poor is always in season, but God wants genuine faithful obedience. Don't just tell Him, show Him! He has people offering lip service and shallow promises every day. God *seeks* obedience from the heart. Obedience is always sacrifice, but sacrifice isn't always obedience. Even though you may become caught up in a chain of events, you are still responsible for your actions and how you participate in those events.

Obedience involves direction and action. Devotion to God is critical; but so is seeking His help with our daily lives. Everyone is given certain strengths and abilities. To be used to their greatest effectiveness, we must place our talents in God's hands, to be used under His influence. As it says on any medical prescription - for best results, use only as directed. Commitment needs control or it can result in tragedy. Ignoring God leads to trouble; rejecting God leads to disaster.

Character and integrity are important traits, but remember, God looks at the heart. Courage and strength are important traits too, but God uses people through their weaknesses. How do you act when no one is looking? Is your loyalty still to God? Can God still see an obedient heart willing to serve, even when you are all alone?

Complete dependence on God yields fruitful results. Successful people acknowledge the role God has played in their lives. Even Satan learned that uncontrolled pride was self-destructive. Small acts of pride or obedience can have a great impact. You will notice that God's plans and purposes are carried out with or without our participation. We benefit most if we cooperate and work within God's will and plan.

God does not promise or guarantee an easy or safe life to those who serve Him. John the Baptist thought standing for truth was more important than life itself. It was. Christ spoke of John the Baptist, "I tell you the truth: Among those born of women there has not risen anyone greater than John the Baptist" (Matthew 11:11). A life invested in serving God and doing what He desires is our greatest accomplishment. If you are willing and available, God can use you. God will seek and find those who truly want to know Him. Make God happy; seek Him every day.

The Bible contains more than stories, history, prophecy, and the life of Christ. In the Bible, God reveals Himself completely to us. Apart from the Bible we would know nothing of God or what He requires of us. Only in the Bible do we discover that God has one eternal overriding concern – you! In the words of Leo Tolstoy, "You think about people, but God thinks about you". As you read the Bible and see men and women used by God in special ways, you see God at work. These men and women were no better or worse than you and I, but God spoke to them. When they responded to Him, things happened.

Sadly, the world is lacking godly leaders. There have always been men of tomorrow, but today their numbers are fewer and fewer. God is still speaking to us today through His word. God is calling you today to be *fellow workmen for God*. God still speaks and calls men to take their place today in the tomorrow He is creating. As we respond, we can be counted as part of God's workmen, a peculiar people, a church for all men - men of tomorrow.

Life is terribly short; what is your decision? Are you acting by faith through obedience in the grace of God? Is it all about you, or will you become part of God's workforce? God kindly requires an answer – as soon as possible, please.

Chapter 12

Finding God in the Chaos

EXTRA, EXTRA, Read all about it...
The World is Coming to an END!

Plane crashes in Egypt - No survivors -
Cause still shrouded in mystery
Heat Index reaches 107 degrees –
Nine more homeless die, totaling 38
Ferryboat takes on water - 289 drown –
Rescuers unable to help
Blood supply found tainted -
Thousands to be tested for AIDS
Forest fires out of control - Over 620 homes lost –
Thousands homeless
Tropical storms create total devastation –
Thousands missing and injured –
Damages estimated in untold billions!

These are grim headlines for any paper, any city, in any country. The world is awash with peril. Your life is exposed to imminent danger. Seen and unseen forces swirl around your little cosmos, waiting to "catastrophize" your existence. You can avoid planes, trains, and subways. You can walk to work, eat organic vegetables, drink the purest bottled water, and use sunscreen rated SPF-150.

Try as hard as you can to reduce your exposure to a deadly world, you cannot. There is no *Safe Place* where you are at peace, where you can deal with anything life throws at you. You are at risk in the womb. The schoolhouse is fraught with bullies. The worksite is perilous and often a minefield. Even a serene nursing home can seem like an oasis, but become a place of despair and solitude and abuse. You are walking a broad path of chaos your entire life.

Can you stop the tiniest blood clot from giving you a crippling stroke? Can you prevent a mosquito from biting you and giving you malaria or the West Nile virus? Can you really expect to live in an environmentally, socially, economically, religiously, politically, and ergonomically correct bubble, and be brazen enough to fear no evil? You cannot prevent evil from brushing up against your daily life. Jesus said, "In this world you will have trouble. But take heart! I have overcome the world" (John 16:33).

Are you afraid of the unknown, the unseen, the unforeseeable, the unimaginable, even the incomprehensible? If you are afraid to take any course of action, afraid to think, even afraid of a leaf dropping, then Satan has you right where he wants you. It does not have to be that way. It is crippling to be paralyzed with fear and indecision. But God didn't give us a spirit of fear and trembling. Quite the opposite, God gave us the ability to address all these mysteries and more – it's called faith.

While the future rushes at us with blinding speed, most people really believe they will make things right with God when they *feel* the time is right or when they have one foot in the grave and their time is at hand. This manner of reckoning allows them to be in denial; seeking pleasure instead of attending to weightier spiritual matters - all while flirting with sin in its various disguises. This manner of life, although commonplace, is deceptive and plays into the devil's strategy of getting you to forfeit your soul. Satan is a predator, stalking the weak and indecisive. Everyone is his prey.

The world copes with uncertainty and chaos in various ways. Through the ages it has been popular to have money saved and diversify your assets. There is a measure of collected wisdom in that manner of thinking. Material needs are more easily determined and planned for than spiritual needs. Many individuals plan for their spiritual condition by putting major decisions off until tomorrow and trusting God to see their good deeds and reward them accordingly. God does not favor procrastination. He requires us to assume some responsibility for our spiritual position and our service to Him.

The world cannot find God in the chaos because the world isn't looking for God. The world puts its hope and faith in bigger armies, hoarding resources, and trusting their governments and economies to build a better future. To the world, God is an anachronism, a distant memory to be found in the Old Testament Jewish Bible. They are gravely mistaken. God has not moved. He still walks among us and seeks our company. The world has moved itself farther away from God.

The Christian has ways to cope with uncertainty and chaos that encourage faith and trust in God and help dispel fear and anxiety. A person of faith knows that God is omnipotent and omniscient, and that whatever we face in this life - uncertainty, danger, or even death - God's grace will be sufficient. We have a vigilant God who will stand between us and danger when we ask for His protection. The apostle Paul told the Corinthian church not to be seized with uncontrollable fear and dread.

> "No temptation has seized you except
> what is common to man. And God is faithful;
> he will not let you be tempted beyond what you can bear.
> But when you are tempted, he will also provide a way out
> so that you can stand up under it."
> 1 Corinthians 10:13

For years you have been captive to your lust, your greed, and your pride. Your appetite never has been satisfied. Sin promises freedom, but it only delivers pain and suffering and ultimately death. We are prisoners of life itself, and we suffer because we live in a fallen world. We do not own the garden anymore. We suffer because we are disobedient. We suffer because we can't change our own hearts. We can expect unanswered prayer if we demand change without inviting God's presence. Martin Luther once said, "I am convinced that when a Christian rightly prays the Lord's prayer at any time…his praying is more than adequate." Are you searching for God, or are you contributing to the chaos? How do *you* find God in the chaos of daily life?

First, you can find God by seeking Him.

You find God by earnestly searching His word, the Bible. Neglecting and rejecting God's word can have immediate and dire consequences. Written over two thousand years ago, it has withstood the ravages of skeptics, philosophers, doubters, and uncommon fools. It is the only cure in solving the bone-crushing problems you face today. The Bible gives us a plan for world peace. The application fails when men will not believe it and obey it. It has been said, "It is not that Christianity has been tried and found wanting; rather, it has been found difficult and not tried."

Your life is pelted incessantly with questions and doubts that demand answers. You can't avoid, hide, or run from them. Why? Because you've tried various escapes before, and they keep coming back. Diversions, you have tried them all – money, work, sex, drugs, rock n' roll - even the lowly television cannot pander to our thirst for divine attention. All these diversions and distractions are forever stalking you. They are relentless on this side of eternity. The Bible serves as a lighthouse warning of the rocks ahead.

"Be self-controlled and alert.
Your enemy the devil prowls around like a roaring lion
looking for someone to devour."
1 Peter 5:8

Understand that your life is perpetually filled with changing circumstances. Forces beyond your control or comprehension are vying for your attention, your allegiance, your very real mortal soul. God whispers to your inner conscience, seek Me, find Me, come dwell with Me. The devil whispers in your ear that you do not have time for all that; eat, drink and be merry for tomorrow you may die. Isn't it odd, either way you are going to die? But one choice leads to your garden identity and life everlasting with our creator, and the other leads to unimaginable pain and suffering. The choice is yours to make, and yours alone. At the present, it's all about you and the decisions you make. In the future, this choice may not be available to you. Are you looking for that narrow gate, or will you be pushed or pulled into eternity?

> "It is a dreadful thing
> to fall into the hands
> of the living God."
> Hebrews 10:31

Second, you can find God in the chaos by His Holy Spirit.

When he was faced with the same circumstances as you, Thomas a' Kempis prayed this simple prayer: "Come Lord, and speak to my heart, communicate to it Your holy will, and mercifully work within it both to will and to do Your good pleasure." Do you, like Martin Luther, feel prayer is enough? Are you seeking the Lord's will like Thomas a' Kempis? Are you making an honest effort to invite God into your life?

Maybe you have always felt that God should be experienced in a personal way, and rightly so. After all, we're just trying to get back to where we came from. What road do you take to go back to the very beginning? The way we are seeking, but resisting with all our pride, is the path to repentance. God has a panacea to meet that very desire within us. The panacea is called The Holy Spirit, whose mission is to aid and abet, if we are so willing.

Jesus told us a great deal about the Holy Spirit. He said, "When he comes, he will convict the world of guilt in regard to sin and righteousness and judgment" (John 16:8). He will do this by various means: through the Scriptures, through the preaching of the gospel, through our conscience, and by the testimony of our Christian friends. He is tireless, relentless, and resourceful in trying to reach you. When you respond to the convictions of the spirit, and believe Jesus Christ to be your Lord and Savior, the spirit gives you a new spiritual life. "He saved us, not because of righteous things we had done, but because of his mercy. He saved us through the washing of rebirth and renewal by the Holy Spirit, whom he poured out on us generously through Jesus Christ our Savior" (Titus 3:5-6). God sent His spirit to draw you back to the creator you seek. You, however, must respond. If you are drowning and refuse help, how else will you be saved?

The Holy Spirit will provide guidance and comfort through the Scriptures. He will guide the believer to seek and find the will of God in everything. He will do all these things and more if...*IF* we yield to His gentle persuasion. "But when he, the Spirit of truth, comes, he will guide you into all truth" (John 16:13). "So I say, live by the Spirit, and you will not gratify the desires of the sinful nature. For the sinful nature desires what is contrary to the Spirit, and the Spirit what is contrary to the sinful nature. They are in conflict with each other" (Galatians 5:16-17).

When you look for answers to life's problems, the Holy Spirit is waiting to calm your deepest fears. If you allow Him, He will restrain evil, convict sin, indwell the believer, and instruct you in godly living. Do you want to remain adrift in the cosmos? Your life is purpose-driven whether you recognize it or not. God will weave events in and out of your life to draw you back to Him. God is addressing this opportunity to help you personally; don't keep rejecting His offer. He can withdraw His offer of grace if you spurn Him too often!

Third, you can find God in the chaos by trusting in God's will.

When Abraham Lincoln was faced with crushing discontentment he said, "I have been driven many times to my knees by the overwhelming conviction that I had nowhere else to go. My own wisdom, and that of all about me seemed insufficient for the day."

The issues facing you are insurmountable - under your own power. When Adam and Eve left the Garden of Eden, they had been stained with sin and required the creator to restore them. They had no hope of returning to their garden. Like you, they needed God's answers to life's needs. Whether you are too religious, anti-religious or semireligious, God will call you to draw close to Him. You can respond or procrastinate, but you cannot escape His care.

It is easy to say to people, trust in God's will, but do you know enough about God's will to follow that instruction? God has been extremely tolerant with our disobedience. Now it is time for us to seek and understand His will for our lives, both in specifics and generalities. One general rule everyone should commit to memory is found in Proverbs.

"Trust in the Lord with all your heart
and lean not on your own understanding;
in all your ways acknowledge him,
and he will make your paths straight.
Do not be wise in your own eyes;
fear the Lord and shun evil."
Proverbs 3:5-7

God delivered an entire nation of millions from cruel bondage and slavery through the leadership of Moses. After leaving Egypt, God saw that the nation needed to know His will for their lives in their newly found freedom. He gave them, and us, the Ten Commandments so they would know of His holiness and what was expected of them. We need reminding that the Ten Commandments, found in Exodus chapter 20, were not guidelines or suggestions or multiple choices: they were just what God intended them to be – commandments! He tried to establish His people on a path of faithfulness and obedience, but it soon became obvious they preferred chaos to holiness and order.

Even the most primitive barbarian knows part of God's will, better known as the Golden Rule: found in Matthew 7:12, "Do to others as you would have them do to you". Most people have heard of the Ten Commandments and the Golden Rule, but what about the direct, specific will of God - the heart of the matter that applies to you and to me? That is found in Paul's letter to those living in Thessalonica.

"Live in peace with each other.
And we urge you brothers, warn those who are idle,
encourage the timid, help the weak, be patient with
everyone.
Make sure that nobody pays back wrong for wrong,
but always try to be kind to each other and to everyone else.
Be joyful always; pray continually; give thanks in all
circumstances,
for this is God's will for you in Christ Jesus."
(Emphasis added)
1 Thessalonians 5: 13-18

God wants us to be submissive to the authorities because they, in turn, will answer to Him. You can find out how by reading Proverbs 8:15-16; Romans 13:1-7 and 1 Peter 2:13-15. The conclusion of following God's will is found in the Book of Ecclesiastes, chapters 12 and 13. If you want just one verse to memorize that encapsulates the role of man, it is this: "Fear God and keep his commandments; for this is the whole duty of man" (Ecclesiastes 12:13).

Everyone knows what to do when there is money in your pocket, your health is good, you have a warm place to sleep, plenty to eat, and you're safe and comfortable. Aside from the obvious, you take it easy and enjoy life – for a while. Until *it* happens. You know, *IT*, that unplanned event that shakes your comfortable world, and reaches down to your very essence. It is when you arrive at a divine intersection.

It might be a death in the family, a divorce, a bankruptcy, an incurable disease, or a chicken bone caught in your throat! Whatever it is, your world will feel like it's falling into an abyss. Its tentacles will grip your very soul and pull you into the chasm. Sorrow reaches up and pulls you into its web. You will get serious indeed and start looking to God for answers. What is your purpose in life, and where is God all of a sudden? It will be a *teachable* moment when it happens. When it occurs, it will be *all about you*. How will you react, what will you do? Cry out to God for help or curse and prepare for the shock wave?

You imagine that nothing like that will happen to you. Do remember those terrible headlines at the beginning of this chapter? None of those disasters suffered by those people was of their own making. Circumstances changed their lives from the outside, but it is God who changes our lives from within. Circumstances dictated their response, but you can respond before the circumstances overwhelm you. Sometimes you see the warning signs approaching and sometimes the sky falls without any notice. Suddenly you are involved and you must respond.

That calamitous experience will affect you in ways you cannot possibly imagine. Your life will take on a new importance. It will bend you, but not break you. It will make you either better or bitter. It is a milestone in life everyone faces, sooner or later. The question should be asked here and now – do you want to face these life changing calamities alone or with supernatural help? Can you prepare for any contingency, or would you like to have a guiding hand, a voice of reason, the Word of Truth to walk you through it?

Remember when Jesus was baptized in the wilderness by John the Baptist? Jesus went into the desert and fasted for forty days and forty nights. After His period of fasting when He was at His weakest, the devil approached and tempted Him three times, and three times Christ rebuffed him by quoting Scripture. Then something very ordinary happened: the Bible records that Satan left Him - *for a season*. Did Satan return? Time and again he returned; just as he continually returns for you. He desires either your soul or to deprive you of your rewards. We would be wise to emulate Jesus, and give Satan nothing but Scriptures.

When you face trouble of epic proportions, where do you turn? When there's anxiety, fear, dread, worry, exhaustion, conflict, or burnout, where do you find the wisdom for making sound decisions? Plan ahead, be changed from within; acknowledge the sovereignty of God over your future. The humanist view, popular in Europe, is that man decides his own future. The Christian view is that God is in control and our future is determined by our relationship with His son, Jesus Christ.

Life is a proving ground that tests your emotional and spiritual limits. Although life is brutally short and filled with chaos, the question everyone must address is how do you deal with the issue of eternity? Life is not random, capricious, or meaningless. It has purpose, substance, and value. Therefore, we should treat it as such. Live in the mystery that God is sovereign and always does what is right. Do not think you can help God decide all of life's twists and turns. If we could know everything about God, then He would not seem so special. Jesus put our brief life into perspective by reminding us of who is in control: "Therefore I tell you, do not worry about your life, what you will eat; or about your body, what you will wear. Life is more than food, and the body more than clothes. Consider the ravens: They do not sow or reap, they have no storeroom or barn; yet God feeds them. And how much more valuable you are than birds!" (Luke 12:22-24).

Fourth, you can find God in the chaos by being faithful and obedient.

The devil entices you away from walking with the Lord. No one is exempt from his attacks, and no one is completely successful in countering those assaults. One thing we cannot do is give up and give in without a struggle. Satan's temptations seek a sympathetic chord in every human heart. Prepare yourself; compass your mind toward heaven, anchor your heart and mind with Scripture. Your efforts will not be perfect, but persist; desire to walk with God through the chaos.

Why wait for a massive hardship that will break and crush you? Face reality now. Life is brief, uncertain, and insignificant without God. A life without God does not count for much. The Bible admonishes and advises us to be heavenly-minded about things. God does not traffic in arrogance, pride, and self-sufficiency. He responds to humility, repentance, and genuine sorrow.

We must set aside our soap operas, our game shows, our situation comedies and dramas and see that there is a real world wasting away. A real world yearning for truth, meaning, and purpose. If we took seriously the truths Jesus espoused, what might happen? We need to exalt the contribution Christ made and let His words and actions guide our destiny.

Have science and technology given us a better world to live in? Are we more secure or more uneasy? We are isolating ourselves from God and from each other. People are hungry for meaning and purpose. Science cannot deliver, and neither can materialism, knowledge, money, or drugs; none of these can replace the peace and love God gives us.

Love is a life choice and a deliberate action. Even in this world wracked with sin, everything Jesus did was supremely loving. Are the choices we make in life displaying our love for Christ? We should love Him because He first loved us (see 1 John 4:19).

Christ's love is evidentiary. He provided us with living proof, as recorded in the gospels. He exemplified dying proof by hanging on that wooden cross. Eyewitnesses testified of His resurrection after three days in the grave. The evidence is severely clear, God chose you from the very beginning. God is currently showing His undying love for you in multiple ways: are you living proof of it? People should be able to see God through your words and actions - if not directly, then at the very least, His reflection!

Love is more than a good warm fuzzy feeling. It is an attitude that personifies Christ. First Corinthians chapter 13 tells us what love is in words that anyone can understand. Love is patient and kind. It also tells us what love is not. It is not proud, rude, self-seeking, and not easily angered. Love does not envy, does not boast, and does not keep a record of wrongs. Love always protects, always trusts, always hopes, and always perseveres. Love never fails. God is love. (see 1 John 4:8)

The Bible mentions several types of love: *philo* (a brotherly love), *eros* (a sensual love), and *agape* (a godly love). There is a love for friends, a love for lovers, and a love that lets someone drive iron spikes through your wrists and feet, then lifts you up to be crucified. For someone else's sin! A wise and gifted teacher once described this unique agape love as ***doing the loving thing, whether you feel like it or not.*** Such a love can only come from the heart of heaven.

"Whosoever does not love does not know God,
because God is love.
This is how God showed his love among us:
he sent his one and only Son
into the world that we might live through him.
This is love:
not that we loved God, but that he loved us
and sent his Son as an atoning sacrifice for our sins."
1 John 4:8-10

Knowing that we can call on God at any moment gives us incredible hope. Knowing that we can rely on His promises gives us incredible assurance.

Hope is real, hope is genuine, hope is the seed that grows for God within every human heart.

"Brothers, we do not want you to be ignorant
about those who fall asleep,
or to grieve like the rest of men, who have no hope."
1 Thessalonians 4:13

Hope is not something to be grasped just with the intellect. It is to be encountered heart to heart, mind to mind, spirit to Spirit! What can happen to you if you neglect the Bible and find yourself thrust into eternity with no hope?

"How shall we escape, if we neglect so great a salvation."
Hebrews 2:3 KJV

You *cannot* neglect God's gift of salvation, because there will be no other gift forthcoming. You cannot trust in your youth; it will fade away and you will find yourself older with even less time to decide. You cannot trust fame and fortune; they will be replaced by someone else soon enough. One day soon, you will see death slowly approaching; it is then you will realize that there is life after death, and that God has been patiently waiting on you! It might be your first or your last warning. Be receptive to God's urging.

You have the ability and privilege to make life-changing decisions, even in the midst of the chaos around you. Today you can escape God's wrath by an act of the will. Decide to follow Christ *now* – do not procrastinate any longer. God has an extensive accounting department. You cannot escape His watchful eye or His providential care. All our feeble efforts to elude Him, or please Him, are being recorded. It is time we quit being so self-centered. We are incessantly seeking the ephemeral. We worship leisure and recreation, beauty and money. This unattainable happiness is diverting our treasure and pulling our hearts with it.

God's favor is reciprocal and conditional. If there is no genuine repentance and no genuine sorrow over our sin, there will be no genuine forgiveness. God is not deceived - He looks at the heart and He knows our intentions.

We search for spiritual counterfeits through reality TV shows, through science fiction movies, and through romance novels that promise happy endings. We are rushing headlong into an abyss and it is high noon with clear skies. God said, "You will seek me and find me when you seek me with all your heart" (Jeremiah 29:13).

Finding God in the life of Christ is not a leap of faith. Jesus was both divine and human. Theologians call this the *hypostatic union*; it is both a mystery and a paradox. It's a mystery beyond our human understanding. Jesus was an obedient child, a carpenter by trade, and a miracle worker without recognition. Like all humans, He was tempted as we are (see Hebrews 4:15) but He knew no sin (see 2 Corinthians 5:21). This sobering mystery can only be apprehended by faith. The skeptics and rationalists have always made this doctrine their stumbling block. You can own it by faith.

In the first Century the Gnostics, the first heretics, claimed that Christ was divine only, without humanity. Today people accept his humanity, but reject His divinity. Jesus said, "Even though you do not believe me, believe the miracles, that you may know and understand that the Father is in me, and I in the Father" (John 10:38). The miracles Jesus performed were His credentials. The world had never seen such signs and wonders. None of the miracles were self-serving. He did not profit from them; they were all done to showcase God's mercy and glory.

You may choose not to believe Jesus or His miracles. Our nation is filled with people seeking God who attend church regularly but are skeptical about everything. They want the comforts of organized religion, but they are secret dissidents who challenge all authority and prefer to commit to nothing. The world chooses rebellion over obedience. Conservatives, liberals, middle-of-the-roaders; they are all just shades of gray. *When* are we going to realize it is not *who is right* - but *what is right*? The Bible is what is right. It is our source of life and our absolute standard. Remember, Jesus said, "Heaven and earth will pass away, but my words [*the Bible*] will never pass away" (Mark 13:31).

A few times in life, God calls you to service. Maybe you are moved by something great or small; whatever it is, it has a really profound effect on you. It touches your hopeful heart. Do not ignore these special moments when they happen. Ask God to lead, be willing to follow; then see God at work. It is that simple - just respond to God's urging. Wherever God guides, God provides.

For six thousand years, God has been giving advice to a perishing world through His word, through His Spirit, and through His only begotten son. God's message has been persistent and steady throughout history. The past can be very seductive, but the past cannot fill your future needs. The Bible makes it clear; it is very important what you believe. It is equally important what you teach your children, because children follow the example set by their parents. There are plenty of bad role models, so set the bar high and pray for them daily.

Some truths are bedrock fundamentals: the virgin birth of Jesus; His death, burial, and resurrection; His place in heaven at present; and His promised Second Coming. Are these issues settled for you? We should know the contents of the Bible, but beware; knowledge is not the same as salvation.

A dog strains at the end of a leash to be free. But strains for freedom to do what? To aimlessly chase rabbits, to tangle with a skunk, to run with abandon across the road and meet the wheels of a racing automobile? It makes no sense to roam in the twilight of uncertainty, danger, and darkness, but we do the same thing.

In the Old Testament, the Israelites strained against the Law of Moses. They found it crippling to their desire to be free and unfettered. Why couldn't they just be left alone to choose their own life-style, make up their own laws, and decide right from wrong for themselves? After all, they had knowledge of their own. Didn't God trust them to do what was right?

That leash, the Law of Moses, represented security and protection from unseen dangers - dangers they hadn't even imagined yet. Adam and Eve learned that lesson in the Garden of Eden. Their freedom to roam anywhere, do anything, and eat anything proved ruinous. We cannot self-govern ourselves without self-discipline. That is why we are walking a path through chaos today.

The whole world is in chaos, but only a small portion of the world is seeking God. People are looking for God everywhere. Some are seeking Him in nature, some are looking for Him through eastern religions, some seek Him in taverns, in music, or through philosophy; some are even searching for God in science. A few hope to find Him through the Hubble space telescope! One thing is for certain; they have found some of His handiwork!

God *can be found* in the chaos. He never promised you that trouble would never touch you. He did promise to guide you, to provide comfort, to give you peace, and to walk with you through any trial – even through the valley of the shadow of death. Psalm 23 gives great comfort to those at the end of this earthly race. Who has been your shepherd? Don't wait to take the Shepherd's hand at the very end, be walking hand in hand from this moment on.

When people were bringing babies and children to Jesus, just to have Jesus touch them, some adults complained but Jesus said, "Let the little children come to me, and do not hinder them, for the kingdom of God belongs to such as these. I tell you the truth, anyone who will not receive the kingdom of God like a little child will never enter it." (Luke 18:16-17)

Could it be that simple? Is that all it takes – childlike faith? The apostle Paul tells us, "It pleased God by the foolishness of preaching [*the gospel*] to save them that believe" (1 Corinthians 1:21 KJV). People are looking for God and seeking the secret to eternal life, and it has been here all along. Printed on paper, in every language, and sold around the whole world under the simple title: *The Holy Bible*! For years, it has been hiding in plain sight; sitting on a bookshelf with cookbooks, novels, and children's books. Just imagine, a book that contains all the mysteries of the universe available to everyone, whenever they desire. What are you waiting for? The Bible is all about you; be all you can be – read it!

The end times are almost here. Are you consumed with the cause of Christ, or is it all about you? The days of your youth are fading, your life is changing, your moment of decision is *now*. God sees your life in total, and He is patient until the end. You must see that God has revealed Himself: by His word, by His love, and by His son.

In the past God spoke by His prophets, but now, in these last days, God's last personal expression is in the person of Christ Jesus. The complete plan for salvation and daily living has been given through Jesus. Jesus Christ is the full revelation of God to man. No more is needed, and no more will be given.

God has done everything possible to show His love for you. In the beginning, it was all about you. Now, it is time to give yourself to God in love, faithfulness, obedience, and service to "show the world that you're really *all about God*."

Chapter Summaries

Chapter One
Your True Identity

Your true identity seeks to walk with God in Eden. We seek God and His love because we are lonely and only God can fill that specific need for companionship. Seek God because He first sought you, love God because He first loved you, and desire to be with Him because He is calling you to come home.

Chapter Two
Seeking Reconciliation

Living in a rapidly changing world should not alienate you from God; instead, it should draw you to Him for security. Once you find peace with God, savor it, nurture it, and grow in it. Pride can thwart God's plans for your life, but obedience and humility can restore the relationship and reconcile you to God.

Chapter Three
Walking on Water

God walked on the water, but we must wade through it. Trouble visits everyone, and how we respond to it is what gets God's attention. We need to involve Him for guidance and direction toward resolution. Difficulties can result from our own actions or from outside influences. Satan can and does send trouble to us. It is not our place to measure the scope of the trial, but we should be obliged to pray and seek God's counsel. We deny God's help when we refuse to allow Him to share in our life, both in joys and sorrows. When troubles seem to overwhelm you, seek someone who needs help and comfort him!

Chapter Four
Letter from Paradise

When God gave us the Bible, it was for everyone - for every nation, for any dispensation – forever. It was a love letter penned by the hand of God. The Bible is the only instrument that reveals our Creator and how He communicates with us. Having stood the test of time and critics, the Bible will remain – even if heaven and earth should pass away. The Dead Sea Scrolls reveal how something old can be new again.

Chapter Five
Presence of Evil

A presence of evil permeates your world. Sin is a contagion that affects all of life. Sin is deceptive and deadly, and an offense to God. Adam and Eve felt the bite of the serpent's lie until their death. God extends His mercy and grace to all: some accept it and receive forgiveness of their sin, and some reject it and await God's judgment. Sin is relentless, but Christ's sacrifice at Calvary is all-sufficient. Jesus is still calling to all sinners, "Come home."

Chapter Six
Decisive Convergence

We are God's creation, made to be near and dear to Him. Our decisions need to be influenced and guided by the Bible. Choosing the direction and content of life brings either shame or glory upon the Lord's name. Decisive convergence is a discipline to master *before* sin entices us. Choose to follow God first, and then learn how to please Him by cultivating your gifts. Give to others what God has given to you.

Chapter Seven
Under the Influence

Sin has separated us from fellowship with God and must be dealt with before the relationship can be restored. Old Testament sacrifices and prophets pointed to a coming Messiah, one who would deal with the sin issue. A profound influence, Jesus would forever change the way the world would view God. From the gospel writers to His apostles, His life would be recorded in minute detail. Verified eyewitness accounts of His miracles and the recorded resurrection provided salvation to those who believed. They were just common men who wrote about an uncommon life.

Chapter Eight
Narrow's the Road

Death is inevitable. Sin is to blame, and we are caught in its grip until released by God's saving grace. Life is a gift from God, and it is not to be wasted or taken lightly. Knowing death could come at any time, we should be prepared for the afterlife and keep our affairs in order. Minimize cognitive dissonance; quit being torn between *loving* this world and *anticipating* God's Kingdom. This world will perish, but heaven is forever. Jesus said he was the only way to heaven. It is a narrow path not traveled by everyone. Everything we need to know about heaven has been revealed to us. Our response is our acceptance or rejection of His offer of eternal life.

Chapter Nine
Angels Among Us

Angels are among us. They fulfill the role of messenger and are busy conducting God's affairs toward humanity. Unique, with a myriad of qualities, they have played many important roles in history and prophecy, and will be feared in events to come. Angels are important, but God is supreme and sovereign. Don't substitute bonding with Christ for an influential fascination with angels.

Chapter Ten
Who's Your Shepherd?

We are curious and have questions about our purpose, our future, our role in life, and about God. The Bible reveals to us everything we need to know about our Creator, our destiny, and ourselves. Our teacher is Jesus Christ and His life, our tutor is the Holy Spirit, and our responsibility is to be diligent and search the Scriptures to learn all we can. God is omnipresent, omniscient, omnipotent, and immutable. The Kingdom of God is coming. The judgment day is coming. What is your disposition? Are you following a form of godliness or are you following God?

Chapter Eleven
Men of Tomorrow

Our hopes and dreams are constantly changing. But one thing should remain consistent - our desire to be like Christ. If our heart doesn't yearn for the things of God, how can our mind? God uses people in spite of their inadequacies. Our lives are built for service - being selfish and self-centered only frustrates and distracts us from doing what God intended. The book of Proverbs gives us incredible insight into how people behave and how they should behave. God needs people who take an interest in Him, not in themselves. Find out what pleases God and seek to accomplish those things. Obedience results from an intimate relationship with God. Be men of tomorrow; serve the living God!

Chapter Twelve
Finding God in the Chaos

The world is rebellious and your life is in constant danger. We all walk a path of chaos, but Jesus said, "...but take heart! I have overcome the world" (John 16:33). God is all-powerful; for any uncertainty we face in life, God's grace will be sufficient and more! Life is filled with circumstances and forces beyond our control. God asks us to do what we can, then turn the rest over to Him. Although the world is filled with chaos, you can find God by simply seeking Him. God has no trouble finding you; do you have trouble finding Him?

Guidance for Your Daily Life

The following Scriptures provide a quick reference for your use as a starting point into a deeper knowledge of the Bible. Whenever you are concerned about one or more of the topics listed, read the quotation cited, then read as much more of the chapter(s) as needed to understand the context. In the concordance of your Bible, search for other references pertaining to the subject. Space has been provided between topics so you may add Scriptures that you find meaningful.

Anger...

"My dear brothers, take note of this: Everyone should be quick to listen, slow to speak and slow to become angry, for man's anger does not bring about the righteous life that God desires." (James 1:19-20)

_____

_____

_____

_____

_____

_____

_____

Assurance...

> "I write these things to you who believe in the name of the Son of God so that you may know that you have eternal life." (1 John 5:13)

_____

_____

_____

_____

_____

_____

_____

Children...

> "Train a child in the way he should go, and when he is old he will not turn from it." (Proverbs 22:6)
>
> "Children, obey your parents in the Lord, for this is right. 'Honor your father and mother' – which is the first commandment with a promise – that it may go well with you and that you may enjoy long life on the earth." (Ephesians 6:1-3)

_____

_____

_____

_____

_____

_____

Church…

> "Keep watch over yourselves and all the flock of which the
> Holy Spirit has made you overseers. Be shepherds of the
> church of God, which he bought with his own blood." (Acts
> 20:28)

_____

_____

_____

_____

_____

_____

Conscience…

> "So I strive always to keep my conscience clear before God
> and man." (Acts 24:16)

_____

_____

_____

_____

_____

_____

Contentment...

"But godliness with contentment is great gain. For we brought nothing into the world, and we can take nothing out of it. But if we have food and clothing, we will be content with that." (1 Timothy 6:6-8)

"Keep your lives free from the love of money and be content with what you have, because God has said, 'Never will I leave you; never will I forsake you'." (Hebrews 13:5)

_____

_____

_____

_____

_____

_____

_____

Courage...

"For God did not give us a spirit of timidity, but a spirit of power, of love and of self-discipline." (2 Timothy 1:7)

_____

_____

_____

_____

_____

_____

_____

Divorce...

"Some Pharisees came to him [*Jesus*] to test him. They asked, 'Is it lawful for a man to divorce his wife for any and every reason?' "Haven't you read," He replied, "that at the beginning the Creator 'made them male and female,' and said. 'For this reason a man will leave his father and mother and be united to his wife, and the two will become one flesh'? So they are no longer two, but one. Therefore what God has joined together, let man not separate." 'Why then,' they asked, 'did Moses command that a man give his wife a certificate of divorce and send her away?' Jesus replied, "Moses permitted you to divorce your wives because your hearts were hard. But it was not this way from the beginning." (Matthew 19:3-8)

_____

_____

_____

_____

_____

_____

Faith...

"Trust in the Lord with all your heart and lean not unto your own understanding; in all your ways acknowledge him, and he will make your paths straight." (Proverbs 3:5-6)

_____

_____

_____

_____

_____

_____

Grace…

"For it is by grace you have been saved, through faith – and this not from yourselves, it is the gift of God – not by works, so that no one can boast." (Ephesians 2:8-9)

_____

_____

_____

_____

_____

_____

Heaven…

"Do not let your hearts be troubled. Trust in God; trust also in me. In my Father's house are many rooms; if it were not so, I would have told you. I am going there to prepare a place for you. And if I go and prepare a place for you, I will come back and take you to be with me that you also may be where I am. You know the way to the place where I am going." (John 14:1-4)

_____

_____

_____

_____

_____

_____

Hell...

> "Enter through the narrow gate. For wide is the gate and broad is the road that leads to destruction, and many enter through it. But small is the gate and narrow the road that leads to life, and only a few find it." (Matthew 7:13-14)

_____

_____

_____

_____

_____

_____

_____

Honesty...

> "Do to others, as you would have them do to you." (Luke 6:31)

_____

_____

_____

_____

_____

_____

_____

Hope…

"Be strong and take heart, all you who hope in the Lord."
(Psalm 31:24)

_____

_____

_____

_____

_____

_____

_____

Judgment…

"For God will bring every deed into judgment, including
every hidden thing, whether it is good or evil." (Ecclesiastes
12:14)

"But I tell you that men will have to give account on the
day of judgment for every careless word they have spoken.
For by your words you will be acquitted, and by your words
you will be condemned." (Matthew 12:36-37)

_____

_____

_____

_____

_____

_____

_____

Patience…

"Be patient, then, brothers, until the Lord's coming. See how the farmer waits for the land to yield its valuable crop and how patient he is for the autumn and spring rains. You too, be patient and stand firm, because the Lord's coming is near." (James 5:7-8)

_____

_____

_____

_____

_____

_____

_____

Prayer…

"The Lord is near to all who call on him, to all who call on him in truth." (Psalm 145:18)

_____

_____

_____

_____

_____

_____

_____

Repentance…

"If we confess our sins, he [*God*] is faithful and just and will forgive us our sins and purify us from all unrighteousness." (1 John 1:9)

_____

_____

_____

_____

_____

_____

_____

Salvation…

"Salvation is found in no one else, for there is no other name under heaven given to men by which we must be saved." (Acts 4:12)

"Jesus answered, 'I am the way and the truth and the life. No one comes to the Father except through me'." (John 14:6)

_____

_____

_____

_____

_____

_____

_____

Satan...

"Put on the full armor of God so that you can take your stand against the devil's schemes. For our struggle is not against flesh and blood, but against the rulers, against the authorities, against the powers of this dark world and against the spiritual forces of evil in the heavenly realms." (Ephesians 6:11-12)

_____
_____
_____
_____
_____
_____

Suffering...

"When times are good, be happy; but when times are bad, consider: God has made the one as well as the other. Therefore, a man cannot discover anything about his future." (Ecclesiastes 7:14)

_____
_____
_____
_____
_____
_____

Temptation...

> "No temptation has seized you except what is common to man. And God is faithful; he will not let you be tempted beyond what you can bear. But when you are tempted, he will also provide a way out so that you can stand up under it." (1 Corinthians 10:13)

_____

_____

_____

_____

_____

_____

_____

Worship...

> "...that at the name of Jesus every knee should bow, in heaven and on earth and under the earth, and every tongue confess that Jesus Christ is Lord, to the glory of God the Father." (Philippians 2:10-11)

_____

_____

_____

_____

_____

_____

_____

Printed in the United States
103204LV00006B/11/P